Behavioral Fitness and Resilience

A Review of Relevant Constructs, Measures, and Links to Well-Being

Sean Robson, Nicholas Salcedo

RAND Project AIR FORCE

Prepared for the United States Air Force
Approved for public release; distribution unlimited

For more information on this publication, visit www.rand.org/t/RR103

Library of Congress Cataloging-in-Publication Data is available for this publication.

ISBN: 978-0-8330-8450-7

Published by the RAND Corporation, Santa Monica, Calif.
© Copyright 2014 RAND Corporation
RAND® is a registered trademark.

Support RAND
Make a tax-deductible charitable contribution at
www.rand.org/giving/contribute

www.rand.org

Preface

U.S. military personnel have been engaged in operations in Central Asia and the Middle East for the past decade. Members of the armed forces also deploy to other regions of the world. Many aspects of deployments have the potential to contribute to individual stress, such as uncertainty about deployment time lines; culture shock in theater; fear of or confrontation with death or physical injury; environmental challenges, such as extreme climates and geographical features; austere living conditions; separation from friends and family members; and reintegration after deployment. Service members and their families also manage other military-related stressors, such as frequent relocations, long work hours, and the additional family separations associated with unaccompanied tours and domestic training exercises. Some service members and their families may cope well or even thrive as they overcome adversity and accomplish challenging tasks. However, some may suffer negative consequences as a result of military-related stressors, such as physical injury, including traumatic brain injury; depression, anxiety, or other mood disorders; post-traumatic stress disorder; spiritual crises; substance abuse; family dysfunction; marital problems and dissolutions; social isolation; and, in extreme cases, even suicide or suicide attempts. With the aim of preventing such deleterious outcomes, rather than simply responding to them, the study of resilience is of paramount importance.

The Air Force offices of Airman and Family Services (AF/A1S), the Surgeon General (AF/SG), and the Deputy Assistant Secretary of the Air Force for Force Management Integration (SAF/MRM) asked the RAND Corporation to help the Air Force develop its programs to promote resiliency among military and civilian Air Force personnel and their families. This report is one in a series of nine reports that resulted from that research effort.

The overarching report, *Airman and Family Resilience: Lessons from the Scientific Literature* (Meadows and Miller, forthcoming), provides an introduction to resilience concepts and research, documents established and emerging Air Force resiliency efforts, and reviews Air Force metrics for tracking the resiliency of Air Force personnel and their families. It also provides recommendations to support the development of resilience initiatives across the Air Force. We use the term *resilience* to refer to the ability to withstand, recover from, and grow in the face of stressors and *fitness*, which is related, as a "state of adaptation in balance with the conditions at hand" (Mullen, 2010).

Accompanying that overarching report are eight supplemental reports that outline the constructs, metrics, and influential factors relevant to resiliency across the eight domains of Total Force Fitness:

- medical

iii

- nutritional
- environmental
- physical
- social
- spiritual
- behavioral
- psychological.

These supplemental reports are not intended to be a comprehensive review of the entire literature within a domain. Rather, they focus on studies that consider the stress-buffering aspects of each domain, regardless of whether the term *resilience* is specifically used. This expanded the scope of the reviews to include a broader range of applicable studies and also allowed for terminology differences that occur across different disciplines (e.g., stress management, hardiness).

In this report, we identify key constructs relevant to behavioral fitness from the scientific literature: sleep, alcohol use, and tobacco use. This review includes construct measures as well as well-being and resilience outcomes. We also review interventions designed to promote behavioral fitness constructs applicable at the individual, unit, family, and community levels.

The results of these reports should be relevant to Air Force leaders who are tasked with monitoring and supporting the well-being of active duty, reserve, and guard Airmen and Air force civilian employees, as well as their families. The results of our studies may also help broaden the scope of research on resilience and help Airmen and their families achieve optimal behavioral fitness.

The research described in this report was conducted within the Manpower, Personnel, and Training Program of RAND Project AIR FORCE as part of a fiscal year 2011 study titled "Program and Facility Support for Air Force Personnel and Family Resiliency."

RAND Project AIR FORCE

RAND Project AIR FORCE (PAF), a division of the RAND Corporation, is the U.S. Air Force's federally funded research and development center for studies and analyses. PAF provides the Air Force with independent analyses of policy alternatives affecting the development, employment, combat readiness, and support of current and future air, space, and cyber forces. Research is conducted in four programs: Force Modernization and Employment; Manpower, Personnel, and Training; Resource Management; and Strategy and Doctrine. The research reported here was prepared under contract FA7014-06-C-0001.

Additional information about PAF is available on our website:
http://www.rand.org/paf/

Contents

Summary

Building on previous work in behavioral health, we define behavioral fitness as conduct, routines, and habits that promote health and the ability to withstand, recover from, or grow in the face of stressors. We identified several areas to include in our review to be consistent with research on important health practices: sleep behaviors, alcohol and drug abuse, and tobacco use. These key behavioral fitness factors, or constructs, are associated with successfully dealing with stress and strain. We address other relevant behavioral health topics in companion reports in this series.

Sleep is critical to physical and psychological functioning, and excessive sleep loss can contribute to chronic health conditions, poor mental health, and reduced adaptability to stress. Moderate sleep loss can significantly impair performance, particularly on cognitive tasks. Interventions for sleep can be broadly differentiated by the severity of the problem. Serious sleep disturbances have been treated using pharmacotherapy and behavior therapy. Minor sleep disturbances can often be addressed by following good sleep hygiene practices, which are also recommended to prevent sleep problems from developing. Examples of these good sleep hygiene practices include going to bed at the same time each night and removing all TVs, computers, tablets, etc., from the bedroom.

Alcohol and drug use disorder can also negatively affect behavioral fitness. In particular, heavy drinking has been strongly linked to many adverse health outcomes. Alcohol use can have stress-buffering effect; however, regular intoxication may present other complications and can lead to addiction. Interventions for drug and alcohol use disorders have focused on both prevention and treatment. In general, research has found that behavioral therapies, which are sometimes combined with medications to treat alcohol and drug addiction, can be effective in treatment. One of the most effective strategies for the prevention of alcohol consumption as well as smoking is to raise prices. Although there may be challenges to implementation, research has shown that the effects of controlling prices are comparatively larger than other prevention policies.

Smoking is associated with the onset of a number of chronic health conditions and can also increase stress and the risk of mood and panic disorders. Smoking cessation is associated with decreased stress and reduced risk of these disorders; however, stress itself may contribute to the maintenance of and relapse into smoking behavior. Interventions for the treatment of tobacco dependence can be classified broadly into counseling and psychosocial interventions, medications, and systems changes (that is, changes in policy, practices, and/or regulations). For psychosocial interventions, general recommendations indicate support for several clinician-directed interventions including screening for tobacco use, encouraging smokers to quit, meeting four or more times with individuals who are in the process of quitting, and providing interventions through different types of clinicians (e.g., nurse, physician, health educator). Although research has shown that medications can also be effective, combining counseling interventions with medication has shown to be even more effective in helping individuals to quit smoking.

A large literature examines health behavior change with respect to sleep, and drug and alcohol use. This literature finds that many factors are associated with health behavior change, including motivation, attitudes, family background, knowledge, health insurance, and social networks. Current thinking suggests that interventions to promote health behavior should target high-risk individuals, and messages should be individually tailored and also use multimodal means of delivery (e.g., in-person, text messages, emails). Ultimately, any attempt to change health-related behavior should be partnered with a realistic expectation about the extent to which the targeted behavior can be changed.

Acknowledgments

This research was sponsored by the Air Force Resilience office and was led by Mr. Brian P. Borda for a significant portion of the study period and by Air Force Surgeon General Lt Gen (Dr.) Charles B. Green, and Mr. William H. Booth, the Deputy Assistant Secretary of the Air Force for Force Management Integration (SAF/MRM).

We would like to thank the action officers from the sponsoring offices for their role in shaping the research agenda and providing feedback on interim and final briefings of the research findings. Those officers are Maj Kirby Bowling, our primary contact from the Air Force Resilience office; Col John Forbes and Lt Col David Dickey from the Air Force Surgeon General's office; and Linda Stephens-Jones from SAF/MRM. We also appreciate the insights and recommendations received from Ms. Eliza Nesmith while she was in the Air Force Services and from Lt Col Shawn Campbell while he served in the SAF/MRM office.

RAND's Sarah Meadows and Laura Miller led the overall research effort on resilience and provided extensive feedback on a previous draft of this manuscript. Donna White and Hosay Salam Yaqub provided valuable assistance formatting the manuscript and assembling the bibliography.

Finally, we would like to thank Sarah Hunter and Robert Bray for taking the time and effort to review and provide guidance on ways to improve the overall quality of this report.

Abbreviations

AUDIT	Alcohol Use Disorders Identification Test
BAC	blood alcohol concentration
CAGE	cut down, annoyed, guilty, eye opener
CBT	cognitive behavioral therapy
CDC	Centers for Disease Control
DAST	Drug Abuse Screening Test
DoD	Department of Defense
DoDD	Department of Defense Directive
HRB	health-related behavior
ICD	International Classification of Diseases
MSLT	Multiple Sleep Latency Test
NIAAA	National Institute on Alcohol and Alcoholism
NIH	National Institutes of Health
PVT	Psychomotor Vigilance Test
RAPS4	Rapid Alcohol Screen 4
RCT	randomized controlled trial
TFF	Total Force Fitness
TWEAK	tolerance, worried, eye-opener amnesia, and K/cut down

1. The Context of This Report[1]

This report is one of a series designed to support Air Force leaders in promoting resilience among Airmen, its civilian employees, and Air Force family members. The research sponsors requested that RAND assess the current resilience-related constructs and measures in the scientific literature and report any evidence of initiatives that promote resilience across a number of domains. We did not limit our search to research conducted in military settings or with military personnel, as Air Force leaders sought the potential opportunity to apply the results of these studies to a population that had not yet been addressed (i.e., Airmen). Further, many Air Force services support Air Force civilians and family members, and thus the results of civilian studies would apply to these populations.

This study adopts the Air Force definition of resilience: "the ability to withstand, recover and/or grow in the face of stressors and changing demands," which we found to encompass a range of definitions of resilience given throughout the scientific literature.[2] By focusing on resilience, the armed forces aim to expand their care to ensure the well-being of military personnel and their families through preventative measures and not by just treating members after they begin to experience negative outcomes (e.g., depression, anxiety, insomnia, substance abuse, post-traumatic stress disorder, or suicidal ideation).

Admiral Michael Mullen, Chairman of the Joint Chiefs of Staff from 2007 to 2011, outlined the concept of Total Force Fitness (TFF) in a special issue of the journal *Military Medicine*: "A total force that has achieved total fitness is healthy, ready, and resilient; capable of meeting challenges and surviving threats" (Mullen, 2010, p. 1). This notion of "fitness" is directly related to the concept of resilience. The same issue of *Military Medicine* also reflected the collective effort of scholars, health professionals, and military personnel, who outlined eight domains of TFF: medical, nutritional, environmental, physical, social, spiritual, behavioral, and psychological. This framework expands on the traditional conceptualization of resilience by looking beyond the psychological realm to also emphasize the mind-body connection and the interdependence of each of the eight domains.

The research sponsors requested that RAND adopt these eight fitness domains as the organizing framework for our literature review. We followed this general framework,

---

[1] Adapted from Meadows and Miller, forthcoming.

[2] The Air Force adopted this definition, which was developed by the Defense Centers of Excellence for Psychological Health and Traumatic Brain Injury (DCoE, 2011).

although in some cases we adapted the scope of a domain to better reflect the relevant research. Thus, this study resulted in eight reports, each focusing on resilience-related research in one of the TFF domains, but we note that not all of these domains are mutually exclusive. These eight reports define each domain and address the following interrelated topics:

- medical: preventive care, the presence and management of injuries, chronic conditions, and barriers and bridges to accessing appropriate quality health care (Shih, Meadows, and Martin, 2013)
- nutritional: food intake, dietary patterns and behavior, and the food environment (Flórez, Shih, and Martin, 2014)
- environmental: environmental stressors and potential workplace injuries and preventive and protective factors (Shih, Meadows, Mendeloff, and Bowling, forthcoming)
- physical: physical activity and fitness (Robson, 2013)
- social: social fitness and social support from family, friends, coworkers/unit members, neighbors, and cyber communities (McGene, 2013)
- spiritual: spiritual worldview, personal religious or spiritual practices and rituals, support from a spiritual community, and and spiritual coping (Yeung and Martin, 2013)
- behavioral: health behaviors related to sleep and to drug, alcohol, and tobacco use (Robson and Salcedo, 2014)
- psychological: self-regulation, positive and negative affect, perceived control, self-efficacy, self-esteem, optimism, adaptability, self-awareness, and emotional intelligence (Robson, 2014).

These reports are not intended to be comprehensive reviews of the entire literature within a domain. Rather, they focus on those studies that consider the stress-buffering aspects of each domain, regardless of whether the term *resilience* is specifically used. This expanded the scope of the reviews to include a broader range of studies and also allowed for differences in the terminology used across different disciplines (e.g., stress management, hardiness). We sought evidence both on the main effects of resilience factors in each domain (i.e., those that promote general well-being) and on the indirect or interactive effects (i.e., those that buffer the negative effects of stress).

Because the Air Force commissioned this research to specifically address individuals' capacity to be resilient, and thus their well-being, our reports do not address whether or how fitness in each of the eight TFF domains could be linked to other outcomes of interest to the military, such as performance, military discipline, unit readiness, personnel costs, attrition, or retention. Those worthy topics were beyond the scope of this project.

Some other important parameters shaped this literature review. First, across the study, we focused on research from the past decade, although older studies are included, particularly landmark studies that still define the research landscape or where a particular line of inquiry has been dormant in recent years. Second, we prioritized research on adults in the United States. Research on children was included where particularly germane (e.g., in discussions of family as a form of social support), and, occasionally, research on adults in other Western nations is referenced or subsumed within a large study. Research on elderly populations was generally excluded. Third, we prioritized literature reviews, meta-analyses, and on-going bodies of research over more singular smaller-scale studies.

The search for evidence on ways to promote resilience in each domain included both actions that individuals could take as well as actions that organizations could take, such as information campaigns, policies, directives, programs, initiatives, facilities, or other resources. We did not filter out evidence related to Air Force practices already under way, as the Air Force was interested both in research related to existing practices and in research that might suggest new paths for promoting resilience. Our aim was not to collect examples of creative or promising initiatives at large but to seek scholarly publications assessing the stress-buffering capacity of initiatives. Thus, in general, this collection of reviews does not address initiatives that have not yet been evaluated for their effect.

Building on the foundation of the eight reports that assess the scientific literature in each domain, RAND prepared an overarching report that brings together the highlights of these reviews and examines their relevance to current Air Force metrics and programs. That ninth report, *Airman and Family Resilience: Lessons from the Scientific Literature,* provides a more in-depth introduction to resilience concepts and research, presents our model of the relationship between resilience and TFF, documents established and emerging Air Force resiliency efforts, and reviews the Air Force metrics for tracking the resiliency of Air Force personnel and their families. By comparing the information we found in the research literature to Air Force practices, we were able to provide recommendations to support the development of initiatives to promote resilience across the Air Force. Although the overview report contains Air Force–specific recommendations that take into account all eight domains and existing Air Force practices, some are applicable to the military more generally and are highlighted at the end of this report.

2. Defining Behavioral Fitness

"Good actions give strength to ourselves and inspire good actions in others."
— Plato, Philosopher

The conference that resulted in the August 2010 special issue of *Military Medicine* collectively defined the eight domains of fitness we address in this report. "Behavioral fitness" was defined in the following way:

> Behavioral health refers to the relationship between one's behaviors and their positive or negative health outcomes. Although there is some overlap between behavioral health and psychological health (indeed, many health behaviors share a relationship with mental health outcomes), this fitness domain incorporates health-related behaviors rather than underlying psychological factors (Bray et al., 2010b).

Behavioral health emphasizes individual responsibility to engage in behaviors and activities that facilitate the maintenance of health or prevent disease or dysfunction (Matarazzo, 1980). Specific topics addressed within behavioral health and by the special issue of *Military Medicine* include alcohol, tobacco, and drug use and abuse; weight; and sleep problems.

Building on this previous work, we define behavioral fitness as conduct, routines, and habits that promote health and the ability to withstand, recover from, or grow in the face of stressors. Consistent with research on important health practices (Gallant and Dorn, 2001; Cutler and Lleras-Muney, 2010), we identified several areas to include in our review: sleep behaviors, alcohol and drug abuse, and tobacco use.[3]

The rest of this report will focus on the research literature that points to the importance of health behaviors for overall health and well-being. To provide a foundation for this review, several search strategies were used. First, scientific databases (e.g., PubMed) were used to locate systematic reviews, monographs, and meta-analyses on the relationship of each of the content areas (e.g., smoking) and their associations with stress and resilience. Primary research studies were also included to clarify a specific perspective or context (e.g., military population). Second, content search terms were

---

[3] We address other relevant behavioral health topics in companion reports in this series. Specifically, we address weight issues in the reports on nutrition, medical, and physical fitness, and we consider hygiene behaviors (i.e., oral hygiene) in the report on medical fitness.

combined to address the different objectives of this report (e.g., measures, scales, evaluation, prevention, treatment, programs, interventions). Finally, we reviewed guidance and reports published by national organizations (e.g., National Institute on Alcohol Abuse and Alcoholism [NIAAA]).

Chapter 3 addresses sleep, Chapter 4 addresses drug and alcohol use, and Chapter 5 addresses tobacco use. Each chapter begins with a brief review of the literature linking the behavior to health and well-being and concludes with contemporary means of measuring the important aspects of those behaviors. Finally, Chapter 6 reviews the literature on promoting positive health behaviors and provides guidance for programs and policies aimed at increasing the quality and quantity of sleep and reducing drug, alcohol, and tobacco use.

3. Sleep

Significance of Sleep

It is interesting to note that researchers have not been able to clearly establish the purpose of sleep (Friedl and Penetar, 2008). Nonetheless, sleep is absolutely necessary (Rechtschaffen, 1998) and decrements in sleep are strongly linked to a wide range of negative outcomes including reduced physical health outcomes and obesity, poor mental health, and decreased job-related performance (Orasanu and Backer, 1996; Friedl and Penetar, 2008; Killgore et al., 2008; Patel and Hu, 2008; Koffel and Watson, 2009). Other reviews of research suggest that sleep is particularly important in cognition and promotes brain plasticity, which supports learning and memory by forming new and lasting connections in the brain (Walker and Stickgold, 2006; Rechtschaffen, 1998).

Indeed, sleep is important to many biological and psychological functions, and reduced sleep can adversely affect these functions. For example, sleep loss can reduce cytokine production (i.e., Interleukin-6), which is a biological function that may lead to decreased immune system functioning (Redwine et al., 2000). In this event, sleep loss will decrease resilience and can weaken a person's ability to adapt to stress. Even more concerning, a review of research indicates that excessive sleep loss can contribute to chronic health conditions, including coronary heart disease and diabetes (Alvarez and Ayas, 2004). Furthermore, a recent meta-analysis of prospective studies with over 1.3 million participants found that both short-duration sleep (less than seven hours) and long-duration sleep (greater than eight hours) is associated with a higher risk of death, although the reasons for these relationships are not fully understood (Cappuccio et al., 2010). However, individual studies suggest possible explanations. For example, one study found that just one night of sleep deprivation was linked to specific indicators of decreased cardiovascular health (Ozer et al., 2008). In terms of long-duration sleep, some researchers have begun to identify possible correlates to stimulate research to better understand this link. Although the direction of causality cannot be determined, several factors including depression, lack of physical activity, and medical conditions were found to relate to long-duration sleep in a cross-sectional epidemiological survey (Patel et al., 2006).

Sleep loss also affects aspects of mental health including mood and emotion regulation. In a review, Walker and van der Helm (2009) present research supporting the conclusion that sleep plays an important function in "the selective modulation of emotional information and emotion regulation" (p. 731). That is, sleep may promote the consolidation and generalization of emotional experiences, whereas sleep loss may increase reactivity to events (e.g., increased irritability). One study of over 25,000 survey participants with chronic insomnia found that these individuals are at a higher risk of developing an anxiety disorder (Neckelmann, Mykletun, and Dahl, 2007).

Sleep deprivation can also severely limit cognitive functioning (Killgore, Balkin, and Wesensten, 2006; Alvarez and Ayas, 2004). In a study of 39 adults, sleep deprivation was shown to result in slower reaction time and decreased hand-eye coordination and accuracy (Williamson and Feyer, 2000). These performance decrements mimic those found from alcohol intoxication. More specifically, researchers found that sleep deprivation of 17.74–19.65 hours (i.e., after waking) corresponded to a blood alcohol concentration (BAC) of 0.1 percent.

Other individual studies have shown that problem-solving abilities (Linde and Bergstrom, 1992), perceived emotional intelligence, and adaptive coping (Killgore et al., 2008) are just a few other factors negatively affected by sleep deprivation that may affect the capacity to be resilient.[4] Not only do those who are sleep deprived have difficulty adapting, they also take greater risks under conditions of uncertainty (Killgore, Balkin, and Wesensten, 2006). Finally, poor decisionmaking, fatigue, and reduced attention from lack of sleep further contribute to reduced performance and increase the risk of accidents (Mitler et al., 1988; Alspach, 2008).

Measuring Sleep Quality and Quantity

Methods for measuring sleep patterns vary in approach and cost. Polysomnograms, which measure several physiological features during sleep (e.g., oxygen in blood, air expelled through nose, chest movements), are typically conducted overnight in a sleep center or sleep lab to help diagnose certain sleep disorders such as narcolepsy or sleep apnea (National Heart, Lung, and Blood Institute, 2012). Considered the "gold standard," the Multiple Sleep Latency Test (MSLT; Carskadon et al., 1986) determines how sleepy someone is by recording how quickly they fall asleep and the stage of sleep during four or five sessions of rest in a quiet room. The MSLT, which requires special equipment and a controlled environment, is not practical for measuring sleep concerns in an operational environment (Balkin et al., 2004) or for general monitoring of sleep problems in a large population (e.g., the Air Force). Strictly in terms of assessing sleepiness-related performance decrements, Balkin et al. (2004) found in a study of 66 commercial vehicle drivers that the Psychomotor Vigilance Test (PVT) (Dinges and Powell, 1985), which is a

---

[4] The ability to be flexible and adapt is considered by many to be a core dimension of resilience (see the companion report on the psychological fitness domain).

reaction time task, was clearly preferable in terms of reliability and sensitivity to sleep loss than several other outcomes measures such as a driving simulator task, speed of serial addition/subtraction, and grammatical reasoning. This particular measure may be useful to aid immediate decisionmaking and delegation of tasks in an operational environment, but it is not useful for measuring typical sleep patterns or chronic sleep loss, as its focus is on the effects of sleep loss rather than sleep quality or quantity.

One alternative for objectively measuring sleep wake patterns and circadian rhythms is actigraphy. Actigraphs are watch-like devices typically worn on the wrist and can be used outside a sleep lab at home, on travel, or while deployed. Using technology such as an accelerometer,[5] an actigraph records motion to document sleep patterns, with the premise that there is more activity or movement during the wake cycle than during sound sleep. In documentation of its practice parameters for the use of actigraphs, the Standards of Practice Committee of the American Academy of Sleep Medicine (2003) asserted that actigraphy is a valid and reliable assessment for healthy adult populations and can be used as an outcome measure for sleep-based interventions. The committee also noted that actigraphy may supplement sleep logs, in which individuals record the number of hours awake and asleep each day. Both actigraphs and sleep logs can be especially useful when observation and other more intrusive methods of assessment are not practical. Although useful in small studies, the cost of actigraphs[6] must be taken into account, however. Sleep logs, on the other hand, are susceptible to well-known problems with self-report data. Although sleep logs are reliable for assessing total sleep time for group data, considerable variability in total sleep time has been found in a study of veterans when comparing sleep logs to actigraphs (Westermeyer et al., 2007).

Questionnaires are more practical for assessing a range of sleep variables in large, diverse populations. A 2006, guide for sleep disorder resources was published, which catalogued 12 sleep variables: "1) sleep duration (e.g., number of hours slept on average night, last night, etc.), 2) sleep quality and satisfaction (slept well, did you get enough sleep?), 3) sleep disorder diagnosis (ICD9 or ICD10 codes),[7] 4) self-reported sleep disorder symptoms (snoring, restless legs), 5) self-reported sleep disorder (insomnia, restless leg syndrome, narcolepsy, apnea, etc.), 6) factors interfering with sleep (asthma), 7) daytime symptoms associated with sleep (fatigue, tiredness, etc.), 8) reports of sleep-related problems as reasons for medication/therapies, 9) reports of sleep-related problems

---

[5] Accelerometers are also used to measure physical activity (see the companion report on the physical fitness domain).

[6] The cost of actigraphs ranges considerably, depending on features, from a few hundred to more than $2,000.

[7] The ICD is the International Classification of Diseases, a standard diagnostic classification system for use by clinicians and epidemiologists.

as reasons for substance abuse, 10) sleepiness, fatigue, drowsiness associated with traffic fatalities, 11) bedtime (when you go to sleep), and 12) sleeping position for infants[8]" (National Institutes of Health; National Heart, Lung, and Blood Institute; and National Center on Sleep Disorders, 2006, p. 4). These variables have been included in large population-based surveys and in sleep scales and questionnaires. Large population-based surveys, such as the National Health and Nutrition Examination Survey, typically include a variety of survey items rather than carefully validated sleep measures. A simple tally of the variables coded by the NIH in population-based surveys indicates that "sleep quality and satisfaction" was the most frequently assessed sleep variable. Moreover, sleep quality has also been found to buffer the effects of stress. Specifically, in a study of adults with fibromyalgia or rheumatoid arthritis, quality sleep was an important resource in protecting individuals from experiencing negative emotions when under stress or in pain (Hamilton, Catley, and Karlson, 2007). Another study found that one particular component of sleep quality, restorative sleep (e.g., feeling refreshed upon wakening), was directly associated with the reduction of chronic widespread pain in a prospective population-based study (Davies et al., 2008). Other researchers have found similar direct benefits of sleep duration and consistency in reducing psychological strain in undergraduate students (Barber et al., 2010).

Although specific items can be drawn from population-based questionnaires to measure sleep, validated sleep measures offer several advantages including knowledge of sleep dimensions being measured, documented reliability information, and established research linking sleep measures to important outcomes. The most common variable assessed in sleep scales is "daytime symptoms associated with sleep" and was identified in 9 out of 13 scales compiled by the National Institutes of Health; National Heart, Lung, and Blood Institute; and National Center on Sleep Disorders (2006). Some scales measure only one variable (e.g., Stanford Sleepiness Scale), whereas others measure several sleep variables. For example, the Pittsburg Sleep Quality Index (Buysse et al., 1989) asks participants about their sleeping behavior as it relates to sleep quality (e.g., "During the past month, how would you rate your sleep quality overall?") and sleep quantity (e.g., "During the past month, how many hours of actual sleep did you get at night?").

Quality and quantity of sleep are affected by a variety of factors, such as medical disorders, age, stress, and the work and home environment (e.g., shift work, deployment, noise). Deployed service members may be particularly vulnerable to poor-quality sleep. In a recent study of deployed U.S. Air Force members, 74 percent of participants

---

[8] The American Academy of Pediatrics recommends placing healthy infants on their backs to reduce the risks of sudden infant death syndrome.

indicated that their quality of sleep was significantly worse while deployed (Peterson et al., 2008). Factors rated as most disruptive were loud noises outside the tent, sleeping on an uncomfortable bed, and worrying about families. Furthermore, sleep quality was especially poor for deployed night-shift workers, who also had to deal with loud noises inside their tent and adjusting to new sleep patterns when rotating shifts. Sleep problems may persist even following reintegration to a home environment. In fact, insomnia has been raised as a primary complaint among some groups[9] of service members returning from Iraq and Afghanistan (McLay, Klam, and Volkert, 2010). Specifically, 41 percent initially reported problems sleeping following deployment to Iraq or Afghanistan, which persisted for a large proportion (36 percent) of those receiving a followup three months later.

Overall, sleep measures range from the more invasive physiological tests to less precise self-reports of sleep quality and quantity. Although physiological tests may be needed to assess for potential medical conditions, questionnaires using self-report will be more practical and cost-effective for monitoring sleep quality and quantity for large groups of personnel in the Air Force. More expensive options (e.g., actigraphy) may also be useful in limited contexts such as for evaluating the effectiveness of specific interventions to promote sleep. Specific policies and interventions to promote sleep are discussed in Chapter 6.

---

[9] According to the authors, most of those screened had been medically evacuated from theater.

4. Alcohol and Drug Use

Defining Alcohol and Drug Use Terms

Many technical terms are found within the scientific literature to describe problematic drinking and drug use. In this chapter, we define the difference between light, moderate, and heavy drinking when discussing research on alcohol use. For research using terms that have a specific clinical definition (e.g., drug abuse, dependence, alcoholism), we use the term drug and alcohol use disorders. Although it is important to differentiate between these clinical terms when making a diagnosis or when selecting a specific intervention, the goal of our report was to provide a broad overview of research associated with all types of alcohol use, misuse, and abuse.

Therefore, we use the term alcohol and drug use disorders to be consistent with definitions provided by the Department of Defense (DoD). Specifically, Department of Defense Directive (DoDD) 1010.4 defines alcohol abuse as "[t]he use of alcohol to an extent that it has an adverse effect on the user's health or behavior, family, community, or the Department of Defense, or leads to unacceptable behavior as evidenced by one or more acts of alcohol-related misconduct" (p. 2). Drug abuse is defined as "[t]he wrongful use, possession, distribution, or introduction onto a military installation of a controlled substance, prescription medication, over-the-counter medication, or intoxicating substance (other than alcohol). "Wrongful" means without legal justification or excuse, and includes use contrary to the directions of the manufacturer or prescribing healthcare provider, and use of any intoxicating substance not intended for human ingestion" (p. 2).

Prevalence of Alcohol and Drug Use

Alcohol use reflects a significant concern for the military. Although heavy drinking[10] in the Air force was found to be significantly lower than in the other military services, the rate in the Air Force was estimated at 14 percent, which has increased significantly from 10 percent from surveys conducted in 2005 (Bray et al., 2009). This is the largest increase in heavy alcohol use in the Air Force during the period from 1980 to 2008. The rate of heavy drinking was related to beliefs about whether their supervisors drank alcohol. More specifically, the rate of heavy drinking in the Air Force was 10 percent for those who believed that their supervisor did not drink alcohol compared to 16

---

[10] Defined "as drinking five or more drinks per typical drinking occasion at least once a week in the 30 days before the survey" (Bray et al., 2009, p. 29).

percent for those who believed that their supervisor did. Binge drinking, which is defined by drinking four or more drinks for women and five or more for men on a single occasion, is estimated to occur among 28.5 percent of Air Force active duty personnel (Stahre et al., 2009). This rate translates into an estimated 4,954,000 binge episodes per year. Additional research on alcohol use in the Air Force suggests that the total number of deployments and the cumulative time spent deployed are positively associated with drinking behavior (Spera et al., 2011).

Although illicit drug use is less prevalent among military personnel than among civilians and has decreased considerably from previous decades, some concerns have been raised regarding prescription drug misuse (Bray et al., 2010a). The 2008 Department of Defense study on health-related behaviors (HRB) among active duty personnel indicated a past-year misuse of pain relievers at a rate of 17 percent, with the strongest predictor of misuse being prescribed a pain reliever previously (Jeffery et al., 2013).

Outcomes Associated with Alcohol Use

Heavy drinking, defined as four or more drinks in a day for women and five or more drinks in a day for men, results in greater risks of a variety of chronic health conditions, including liver disease, heart disease, sleep disorders, depression, stroke, and several types of cancer (U.S. Department of Health and Human Services, 2010). Alterations to the immune systems have been linked to excessive alcohol use and some chronic health problems (Cook, 1998). Heavy alcohol use has also been identified as a serious problem for the military resulting in higher risk levels for alcohol-related problems including lost productivity (Mattiko et al., 2011). Alcohol use has also been extensively linked to increased risk of accidents and errors in studies of military personnel and civilians (Bell et al., 2000; Streufert et al., 1992; Thompson, Kao and Thomas, 2005). Estimates suggest that alcohol is a factor in as many as 40 percent of fatal motor vehicle crashes, suicides, and fatal falls (U.S. Department of Health and Human Services, 2010). In an extensive study to determine the relative risk of alcohol use, Borges et al. (2006) found an increased risk of injuries from alcohol consumption that was not modified by age or gender. That is, the relative risk of injury was consistent for males and females and individuals of different ages. As expected, however, there were greater overall risks of injury for those with alcohol disorders involving more frequent episodes of drinking.

Although the relative risk of injury may be equivalent for males and females, data from a large cross-cultural analysis show that men are not only more likely to drink than females but will drink greater amounts, more regularly, and will experience more adverse consequences (Wilsnack et al., 2000). These gender differences in drinking behavior also appear in military samples. In a study using data from the 1998 Department of Defense survey of HRB, which included 17,264 military personnel, Thompson et al. (2005) indicated that 9 percent of males and 3 percent of females were intoxicated on more than one day each week. Furthermore, frequent episodes of alcohol intoxication were related to increased sexual risk-taking (i.e., number of sexual partners) among both males and females.

A popular belief held by many is that consuming alcohol can help deal with stress. Indeed, such stress-reactive drinking has been explored in a variety of contexts, including the military. For example, Blume et al. (2010) found some support for a positive relationship between general stress and drinking behavior among Army personnel. More specifically, the younger and nonactive duty (i.e., Reserve and National Guard) soldiers who experienced more general stress were more likely to consume alcohol following deployment. Other large-scale epidemiological research has also shown that individuals who begin drinking at an early age (younger than 15) are more likely to drink after experiencing a stressful life event (Dawson, Grant, and Li, 2007).

Consistent with popular views that alcohol can help people cope with stress, experimental studies have recently shown that alcohol has a stress-dampening response on both self-report and physiological measures of stress (Moberg and Curtin, 2009; Sher et al., 2007). The effects of alcohol on stress reactivity may partly function by reducing anxiety, vigilance, and attention. These anxiolytic effects may be beneficial in the short term; however, regular periods of intoxication can lead to adaptation and ultimately higher levels of anxiety upon cessation of alcohol use (Moberg and Curtin, 2009). Therefore, although alcohol may help to reduce stress in the short term, repeated bouts of intoxication may lead to other negative outcomes including an increased risk of addiction.

Outcomes Associated with Drug Use

Reviews of empirical research show that drug addiction has been extensively linked to stress (Sinha, 2001, 2008). In particular, there is well-documented research demonstrating a positive association between both acute and chronic stress and vulnerability to addiction. Some specific types of stressors that predict addiction risk include loss of a parent, sexual abuse, and unfaithfulness of a significant other (Sinha, 2008). Early life stress (e.g., childhood maltreatment) is also a significant predictor of later addiction. Despite this increased risk, many individuals exposed to early life stress do not develop addiction, suggesting that resilience factors (e.g., social relationships) may be important moderators of the stress-addiction linkage (Enoch, 2011).

Although drug use is most widely associated with negative outcomes, drug use in certain contexts can produce positive outcomes. However, an examination of specific controlled substances—both recreational and prescribed drugs that can be used to manage or reduce stress—is beyond the scope of this review. Law prohibits the use of controlled substances, unless prescribed by a doctor. Furthermore, the majority of research examining prescribed medications targets the treatment of clinical disorders (e.g., anxiety, depression) and pain, which was not the focus of our research.

Identifying Drug and Alcohol Use Disorders

Drug use disorders concern both the use of illicit drugs as well as the misuse or abuse of prescription drugs. Research literature examining the trends from two national surveys in prescription drug abuse showed increases in drug use disorders,[11] specifically for sedatives and opioids (McCabe, Cranford, and West, 2008). Additional concerns were raised by the fact that a small percentage of those abusing prescription drugs received treatment. The military has also identified increases in reported prescription drug use in recent years. The DoD HRB survey indicated that illicit drug use among military personnel has declined over the years to a relatively low level (3 percent), whereas prescription drug misuse has increased from 4 percent in 2005 to 11 percent in 2008 (Bray et al., 2010a). However, it should be noted that the surveys used different wording to improve the clarity of the questions, making it difficult to directly compare responses. Nevertheless, the 11 percent reported in the 2008 survey reflects a significant concern for the military.

Similar to sleep measures, alcohol and drug use can be measured using validated screening instruments or specific items from population-based questionnaires, or objectively using breathalyzers, blood, or urine analysis, which can be used to determine blood alcohol concentration (BAC). Although some similarities to the broad categories of sleep measures can be made, drug/alcohol abuse measures are different in that they may include questions about illegal behaviors and may produce more socially desirable responses, particularly when individuals perceive that negative consequences may occur as a result of their responses. Guiding measures of alcohol use are definitions of a "standard" drink, heavy drinking, and binge drinking. The NIAAA (2004) defines binge drinking as five or more drinks for a typical man and four or more drinks for a typical

---

[11] Drug abuse was defined to be consistent with the criteria established in the *Diagnostic and Statistical Manual*: DSM-IV) (American Psychiatric Association, 2010), which requires at least one positive response for abuse within the past year. Dependence was defined as a positive response to at least three of the seven dependence criteria. An updated definition has been adopted in the most recent DSM-V to combine abuse and dependence into a single diagnosis, termed substance use disorder, to better reflect patient symptoms.

woman within a two-hour period, which is the amount of alcohol consumption that raises blood alcohol concentration to 0.08 percent or more. However, it should be noted that the number of drinks consumed to reach this concentration will vary across individuals due to a number of factors such as age, amount of food eaten before drinking, and weight. However, only recently have similar definitions been developed for binge drinking among children and adolescents. According to Donovan (2009), binge drinking can be defined as three or more drinks for children between ages 9 and 13 and for girls ages 14 to 17 . For boys ages 14 to 15, binge drinking can be defined as four or more drinks and five or more drinks for boys ages 16 to 17. Binge drinking is a particular concern in children as it increases the risk of later alcohol abuse and dependence (DeWit et al., 2000; Dawson et al., 2008; Rothman et al., 2008).

Several instruments for screening alcohol problems, which can be interviewer- or self-administered, have been developed. Items on these questionnaires examine both alcohol use and dependence and the effects of alcohol use. For example, the CAGE[12] (Ewing, 1984) contains four questions: C - Have you ever felt you should cut down on your drinking? A - Have people annoyed you by criticizing your drinking? G - Have you ever felt bad or guilty about your drinking? E - Have you ever had a drink in the morning to get rid of a hangover? Another popular instrument is the Alcohol Use Disorders Identification Test (AUDIT) (Saunders et al., 1993), which contains ten items (e.g., How often do you have a drink containing alcohol? How often do you have six or more drinks on one occasion? Have you or someone else been injured as a result of your drinking?). An abbreviated version containing three items, the AUDIT-C, has also received support as an effective screening tool (Dawson et al., 2005; Bradley et al., 2007).

In a study comparing three screening instruments in adolescents, Kelly et al. (2002) concluded that the AUDIT was a better choice for screening alcohol problems than the CAGE or a modified version of the TWEAK[13] (Saunders et al., 1993). Specifically, the AUDIT has superior internal consistency and was the only instrument in which scores were significantly different for those adolescents with positive and negative screens on a breathalyzer test. In a similar study on adults, the CAGE and the Rapid Alcohol Screen 4 (RAPS4) were directly compared on their sensitivity and specificity for identifying alcohol problems. This study (Cherpitel, 2002) found that the RAPS4 outperformed the CAGE for both alcohol abuse and dependence, which was defined by a more extensive set of items (n = 24) similar to those used in the Composite International Diagnostic Interview. To improve sensitivity of the RAPS4 for alcohol abuse, the authors

---

[12] CAGE stands for cut down, annoyed, guilty, eye-opener, which refer to each of the questions.

[13] TWEAK stands for tolerance, worried, eye-opener, amnesia, and K/cut down, which refers to topics covered in the questionnaire.

recommended adding quantity-frequency questions, "drinking five or more drinks on at least one occasion during the last year and drinking as often as once a month during the last year" (p. 1687). Consistent with this finding, the NIAAA suggests to include a minimum of three questions to measure people's patterns of alcohol use: "[s]pecifically, a measure of frequency of heavy drinking (five or more standard drinks within a two-hour period for men; four or more for women), and standard questions about frequency of alcohol use and typical number of drinks per day when alcohol is used, are necessary to adequately describe drinking patterns and total volume of alcohol consumed" (NIAAA, 2003). Although this represents the minimum number of questions, additional questions can be added to increase sensitivity to alcohol use disorders.

Similar screening tools have also been used to measure drug use. Drug use can be objectively measured using toxicology screens. However, to determine patterns and consequences of drug use, screening instruments such as the Drug Abuse Screening Test (DAST) have been developed (Skinner, 1982). The DAST is a self-report instrument, which contains 28 items[14] reflecting drug use and the effects of drug use (e.g., "Do you use drugs on a continuous basis?"). A comprehensive review indicated that the DAST demonstrates acceptable validity and reliability, can be used for both research and clinical applications, and is appropriate for a variety of populations (Yudko, Lozhkina, and Fouts, 2007). An abbreviated version containing ten items, the DAST-10, has also received support as an effective screening tool (Yudko, Lozhkina, and Fouts, 2007).

Drug and alcohol use are also measured concurrently in population-based surveys. Three major surveys, sponsored by the U.S. Department of Health and Human Services, regularly report drug and alcohol consumption rates in the United States: (1) Monitoring the Future, (2) National Survey on Drug Use and Health, and (3) Youth Risk Behavior Survey. These surveys are quite extensive and include very specific questions regarding the type of alcoholic beverage (e.g., beer, wine) and drug (e.g., marijuana, cocaine), date of last consumption, age of first consumption, and frequency of use.

Formal diagnoses of alcohol dependence and drug abuse can be made using a larger set of items from structured diagnostic interviews. For example, the Composite International Diagnostic Interview, developed by the World Health Organization, contains several sections for substance abuse (Wittchen et al., 1991; Wittchen, 1994). These sections address alcohol abuse, alcohol dependence, drug abuse, drug dependence, and nicotine dependence.

Toxicology screens, used by the military as part of its drug testing program (DoDD 1010.16; Air Force Instruction 44-120), represent another method for monitoring and detecting drug and alcohol use. By examining samples from blood, urine, or hair, a

---

[14] Shorter forms of the DAST, with acceptable reliability, have been developed.

toxicology screen can indicate the type and approximate level of both prescribed and non-prescribed drugs. According to the U.S. National Library of Medicine, these screens must be performed within a certain timeframe when the drug is still detectable in the body. Some substances such as alcohol can be detected for only a short period of time following consumption (i.e., three to ten hours); whereas, other substances when used heavily may be detected for as long as 11 weeks (e.g., Tetrahydrocannabinol) (U.S. National Library of Medicine, National Institutes of Health, 2011). In addition to time limitations for some substances, other research has raised concerns that tampering can lead to inaccurate urine drug screening results (Jaffee et al., 2007). The effectiveness of these tampering methods varies according to several factors, including drug concentration in the urine, the methods and type of drug screen used, and the adulterant used to avoid detection. To minimize the risk of tampering, SAMHSA (2004) recommends that laboratories perform checks to identify if certain characteristics of the urine sample, such as creatine, produce normal values.

Overall, the research shows that alcohol, particularly heavy drinking, and drug use can result in negative outcomes. These risks, including alcohol and drug addiction, are increased with exposure to stress. To measure alcohol and drug use, research has largely focused on self-report measures for the purpose of screening and diagnosing abuse. Objective measures, such as toxicology screens, overcome some of the limitations associated with self-report measures but present additional limitations depending on the drug type and the potential for tampering.

5. Smoking

Prevalence of Smoking

The adverse effects of tobacco use are well known, and prevalence rates in the United States continue to decline. Recent survey results[15] estimated the prevalence of smoking at 31 percent in 2008 across all services, which steadily decreased from 1980 to 2002 and remained relatively stable from 2002 to 2008. However, there are significant differences in tobacco use among service members, with the lowest prevalence among Air Force personnel (23 percent). The HRB results also show that approximately 14 percent began smoking since joining the Air Force. Although the Air Force has compared favorably against the other services, tobacco use remains a concern because of its short- and long-term effects on health and productivity.

Smoking, Stress, and Performance

Tobacco use is regarded as the "single most important preventable cause of death in our society" (Marcus et al., 1993). The evidence is clear: Tobacco use is a cause of many chronic health conditions including cancer, cardiovascular disease, respiratory disease, pulmonary disease, gastrointestinal disease, reproductive disturbances, and oral disease (U.S. Department of Health and Human Services, 2004). Tobacco use has also been linked to increased stress, despite common arguments that smoking relieves tension. In a landmark review, Parrott (1999) discusses several lines of research demonstrating that smokers typically report higher levels of stress and that the cessation of smoking is associated with lower levels of stress. Furthermore, Parrot (1999) reviews evidence showing that adolescents experience more stress as they begin smoking more regularly. More recent evidence further supports these findings. For example, a study using data from the National Comorbidity Survey (Kessler, 1995) found that smoking increased risks of mood and panic disorders (Breslau, Novak, and Kessler, 2004). The cessation of smoking was related to reduced risks, with increasing reductions in risk as time passed since quitting. Higher smoking rates and lower quit rates among individuals with a psychiatric disorder have been well documented in the research literature (cf., Ziedonis et al., 2008). In another review, Kassel et al. (2003) argue that stress may contribute to the maintenance and relapse of smoking. Moreover, they conclude that the relationship between stress and smoking is not necessarily direct and is likely affected by a variety of

---

[15] Data provided from 2008 Department of Defense survey of HRB (Bray et al., 2009).

contextual factors including gender, social influences, and prior mood state. Among the factors linked to tobacco use, prior mental health has been consistently identified.

Tobacco use has also been directly linked to military readiness and performance. In its report on tobacco use, the National Research Council (2009) updated findings from a comprehensive report on tobacco and readiness conducted for the U.S. Army Aeromedical Research Laboratory (Dyer, 1986). In combination, these reviews indicate that smoking impairs physical strength and endurance, reduces night vision, and contributes to hearing loss. Smoking has been linked to an increased risk of injury, accidents, and lost workdays as a result of illness. Not only does smoking have direct effects on health, but it also affects the ability to heal from wounds. Smoking cessation (withdrawal) also produces certain risks by affecting vigilance, information processing, and reaction time.

Although a number of factors appear to contribute to tobacco use (e.g., genetics, mental health, biology), social factors also play an important role. In a population-based survey of all entering USAF military basic trainees (1995–1996), Haddock found that social influences such as trainees' ratings of the social attractiveness of smoking were the strongest factors driving tobacco consumption (Haddock et al., 1998). According to the National Research Council (2009), perceived stress and boredom are also related to tobacco use, especially among deployed service members.

Measuring Smoking

The measurement of tobacco use has primarily been conducted in large, population-based surveys. For example, the Global Adult Tobacco Survey published by the Centers for Disease Control (CDC) evaluates several key components of smoking and smokeless tobacco use. The key questions address patterns and frequency of use, former consumption, age of initiation, nicotine dependence, and frequency of quit attempts. In addition, the survey asks about strategies used to quit, exposure to secondhand smoke, and perceptions about the health effects of tobacco use. Similar questions have also been used to measure tobacco use in adolescents. For example, the Youth Risk Behavior Surveillance System questionnaire asks about smoking behavior, including frequency and intensity of use, intentions of smoking, age of initiation, and smoking cessation (Marcus et al., 1993).

In the military, the DoD requires that the armed services implement guidelines presented in the Veterans Administration (VA)/DoD *Clinical Practice Guideline for the Management of Tobacco Use*. To adhere to this guideline, service members must be asked about tobacco consumption during their physical and dental checkups. The HRB, which is conducted for the DoD, also measures smoking prevalence using questionnaires.

Specific questions on the HRB include use of cigarettes, reasons for starting smoking, intentions to quit smoking, and actual attempts to quit.

Overall, a wide range of topics and questions has been used to address smoking. The most appropriate questions will largely depend on measurement goals and objectives. At a minimum, questions should include the frequency and intensity of use. Other specific questions can be included to aid in the development of programs and initiatives to support smoking cessation (e.g., strategies used to quit).

Although self-report surveys are inexpensive and easy to implement, these measures are likely to underestimate the true rates of smoking in the Air Force. The most accurate way to determine tobacco smoke exposure is to measure continine, a biomarker found in body fluids such as saliva (Gorber et al., 2009). Consequently, cotinine is often used as a benchmark to determine the validity of self-report measures of smoking. Studies evaluating the concordance between self-report measures and continine have been mixed, indicating that self-report measures may be valid in some contexts. For example, a study of military veterans found that self-reported tobacco use was mostly accurate but produced a misclassification rate of 21 percent among self-reported quitters (Noonan, Jiang, and Duffy, 2013). These results underscore the importance of validating self-report measures of tobacco use against direct measures such as continine to ensure that accurate rates are being documented for different subgroups.

6. Promoting Behavioral Fitness

Extensive research has examined programs and interventions for the prevention and treatment of tobacco, alcohol, and drug abuse. Somewhat less research has been conducted on interventions for sleep. In the next section, we will provide a broad overview of the interventions and programs shown to be most effective in effecting health behavior change in general and then more specifically for each behavioral issue. Although the focus of our discussion emphasizes quantitative and systematic reviews to provide an overview of effective interventions, we provide a limited review of efforts specific to the military and the Air Force. Additionally, distinctions are made between prevention and treatment whenever possible. Some interventions, such as those focused on general health behavior change, may target both prevention and treatment.

General Health Behavior Change

Health behavior change has been addressed from many different perspectives. Central to many of these perspectives is the goal of persuading individuals to adopt healthier behaviors. According to the Institute of Medicine, the most effective strategies focus on high-risk individuals and are intensive (National Research Council, 2000). Such a strategy might include communication that is personalized and targeted at a high-risk individual. Indeed, research from a large meta-analysis of 57 separate studies confirmed that tailored messages are effective in promoting behavior change and are more effective than generic messages (Noar, Benac, and Harris, 2007). Tailored messages involve providing feedback and information, which is based on some sort of individualized assessment. Although health care professionals can deliver these messages in person, Noar, Benac, and Harris (2007) argue that computer-based algorithms can be used to generate individualized feedback and information, which enables additional opportunities to promote behavior change across targeted populations.

Sleep Interventions

Interventions for sleep can be broadly differentiated by the severity of the problem. Serious sleep disturbances have been treated using pharmacotherapy and behavior therapy. According to the National Sleep Foundation (undated), insomnia may be treated by a combination of behavioral therapies and possibly combined with sleep medication when behavioral therapies alone are ineffective. Behavior therapy is grounded in the understanding that individuals will engage in a variety of maladaptive strategies to restore normal sleep patterns. Two of these strategies are particularly noteworthy: (1) staying in bed longer by either going to bed earlier or staying in bed later and (2) staying in bed while awake (Perlis et al., 1997). These maladaptive strategies may be mutually reinforcing, ultimately leading to conditioned arousal in bed rather than restful sleep. In a meta-analysis examining insomnia, findings indicated comparable short-term outcomes for both pharmacotherapy and behavior therapy (Smith et al., 2002). In a related meta-analysis with a focus on psychological interventions, similar conclusions were drawn that each psychosocial intervention was similarly effective in treating insomnia (Murtagh and Greenwood, 1995). Among the treatments examined in this study were relaxation (e.g., muscle relaxation, imagery relaxation), stimulus control, sleep restriction, and combination treatment therapies. Slightly different conclusions, indicating that stimulus control and sleep restriction were most effective, were made in an earlier meta-analysis (Morin, Culbert, and Schwartz, 1994).

Minor sleep disturbances can often be addressed by following good sleep hygiene practices, which are also recommended to prevent sleep problems from occurring. According to the International Classification of Sleep Disorders (2001), inadequate sleep hygiene is affected by "various habits and activities of daily living that may promote a sleep difficulty" (p. 73). These habits, generally under the control of the individual (or parents), fall into two general categories. The first category represents behaviors and habits that increase arousal such as drinking caffeine late in the day and staying out late at night. Levels of arousal can also be affected by environmental factors such as noise, excessive light, temperature, and disruptions in the middle of the night from children or pets. Despite the potential for exercise to increase arousal levels, experimental studies and self-report surveys are inconsistent with common guidelines to avoid exercising within four to six hours of bedtime (Youngstedt and Kline, 2006; Myllymaki et al., 2011). In fact, studies regularly find that exercise is associated with better sleep (Youngstedt and Kline, 2006).

The second category of behaviors that contribute to poor sleep quality are those that disrupt the development of consistent sleep patterns, otherwise known as sleep organization. Examples of behaviors that may inhibit effective sleep organization include spending too much time in bed, going to bed at different times, getting up at different times, and taking long or multiple naps during the day. Alcohol in high doses has also been extensively linked to sleep disturbances (Roehrs and Roth, 2001). Recommendations to promote good sleep hygiene are well grounded in research demonstrating moderate to strong relationships between sleep hygiene and sleep quality (LeBourgeois et al., 2005; Brown, Buboltz, and Soper, 2002). These and related findings have led the CDC to recommend several simple tips for practicing good sleep hygiene (CDC, 2010):

"Go to bed at the same time each night, and rise at the same time each morning;

"Sleep in a quiet, dark, and relaxing environment, which is neither too hot nor too cold;

"Make your bed comfortable and use it only for sleeping and not for other activities, such as reading, watching TV, or listening to music;

"Remove all TVs, computers, and other "gadgets" from the bedroom;

"Avoid physical activity within a few hours of bedtime; and,

"Avoid large meals before bedtime."

Research has also indicated that knowledge of good sleep hygiene is associated with sleep patterns and behaviors, which subsequently is related to sleep quality (Brown, Buboltz, and Soper, 2002), and that a program to provide sleep hygiene education can improve sleep quality (Chen, Kuo, and Chueh, 2010). However, knowledge of sleep hygiene may not be sufficient for improving sleep in some environments, where an organizational culture restricts opportunities for adequate sleep. For example, an education program for medical interns, for whom sleep deprivation has been widely acknowledged, was not effective in increasing the amount of sleep (Arora et al., 2007). Consequently, sleep education programs may need to be supplemented with efforts to promote a culture that supports effective sleep hygiene.

Drug and Alcohol Use Interventions

The treatment and prevention of substance abuse has been informed by several different perspectives including behavioral therapies, psychosocial factors, and family systems approaches. An evaluation of treatments designed for specific drug classes (e.g. opioids) or drugs (e.g., Mandrax) beyond alcohol and nicotine (i.e., smoking) were outside the scope of this review. Consequently, this review focuses on systematic reviews and meta-analyses examining treatment and prevention of drug and alcohol use disorders more broadly.

Treatment for Drug and Alcohol Problems

In a recent review, Carroll and Onken (2005) discuss the effectiveness of several behavioral therapies for the treatment of drug abuse, including family interventions, contingency management, and cognitive behavioral therapies.

The inclusion of family members in treatment is a central component of family and couples therapy, which has been used to address both drug and alcohol problems. This approach builds on the power of social support and includes the use of abstinence contracts, skills training, and communication training. In a large meta-analysis of 1,571 cases, family therapy was shown to be an effective treatment for drug problems with superior results compared to individual counseling (Stanton and Shadish, 1997). The prevention of alcohol use in children and adolescents may also be addressed through a variety of family interventions. Programs targeting children are based on the premise that "[a]dolescents model their behavior after their parents' patterns, contexts, attitudes and expectancies of consumption" (Smit et al., 2008). The common features of family and couples therapy, similar to family therapy for drug abuse, include communication skills training, problem-solving, parenting skills, and rule-setting. In a meta-analysis examining random controlled trials for family interventions, Smit et al. (2008) concluded that family interventions are an effective long-term approach to reducing the amount of alcohol consumption in adolescents. However, generalizing from family therapy interventions is problematic in that interventions often contain multiple components, making it difficult to determine which factors are most essential.

Another type of behavioral intervention, contingency management, builds on the foundations of operant conditioning, which rewards target behavior with positive reinforcement. For example, in return for a clear drug screen, participants are provided with desired goods, services, or vouchers. The interventions have proven to be quite effective while rewards are provided (Dutra et al., 2008); however, once the they are removed, the positive effects begin to dissipate. Another concern with this approach is the high cost of implementing regular drug screenings and providing valued rewards.

Cognitive behavioral therapy (CBT), a type of psychosocial intervention, builds upon operant conditioning principles, in addition to social learning theories. This approach is defined by Carroll (1998) and Marlatt and Gordon (1985) by "1) an emphasis on functional analysis of drug use, i.e., understanding drug use within the context of its antecedents and consequences, and 2) skills training, through which the individual learns to recognize the situations or states in which he or she is most vulnerable to drug use, avoid those high-risk situations whenever possible and use a range of behavioral and cognitive strategies to cope effectively with those situations if they cannot be avoided" (as cited in Carroll and Onken, 2005, p. 1454). Empirical support was provided for CBT in a recent meta-analysis (Dutra et al., 2008), which also found that combining CBT with contingency behavioral therapy may yield even stronger effects. Similar methods have been used to treat such high-risk behaviors as gambling (Pallesen et al., 2005).

Another type of psychosocial treatment, motivational interviewing, was evaluated in a more recent Cochrane review (Smedslund, 2011). Motivational interviewing, a method of counseling designed to facilitate a client's intrinsic motivation to change, was found to have its strongest effect soon following the intervention. The effects on drug abuse and dependence were progressively weaker at short-, medium-, and long-term followup.

Psychosocial interventions have also been used for the treatment of individuals with alcohol problems. A narrative review of 23 randomized controlled studies found that well-defined psychosocial treatments are effective for treating alcohol problems (Berglund et al., 2003). For example, the effectiveness of brief interventions, which vary in length from 5–60 minutes, were systematically reviewed in study of 27 randomized controlled studies designed to reduce alcohol consumption (Berglund et al., 2003). Findings suggest that although most brief interventions decreased alcohol consumption up to two years, additional studies are needed to determine the effect beyond this time frame as well as the effectiveness of using brief interventions during routine health checkups.

Overall, behavioral therapies can be effective in treating drug and alcohol use disorders. According the National Institutes on Drug Abuse (2012), "[b]ehavioral therapies can help motivate people to participate in drug treatment, offer strategies for coping with drug cravings, teach ways to avoid drugs and prevent relapse, and help individuals deal with relapse if it occurs" (p. 9). This type of therapy can sometimes be used in conjunction with medications that are available to treat both alcohol (e.g., disulfiram, naltrexone) and drug (e.g., methadone, buprenorphine) addiction. The National Institutes on Drug Abuse provides additional information, including the effectiveness, of these drug treatments.

Prevention of Drug and Alcohol Use Disorders

In a recent review of DoD policies and programs designed to address substance use disorders, the Committee on Prevention, Diagnosis, Treatment and Management of Substance Use Disorders in the U.S. Armed Forces identified two broad classifications of prevention of drug and alcohol problems (Institute of Medicine [IOM], 2013). The first classification of prevention strategies focuses on addressing specific individual needs and behaviors. Among the committee's recommendations to improve efforts to address these needs include focusing on risk factors (e.g., number of deployments) and protective factors (e.g., family support). The committee further emphasizes the importance of using evidence-based programs and practices such as those listed in the National Registry of Evidence-Based Programs and Practices. Finally, programs should ensure that they are age appropriate, are delivered in appropriate settings (e.g., home, school), and provide standardized training to those delivering the program to ensure consistent implementation of important program elements.

The second classification of prevention strategies reviewed by the committee attempts to change or shape community norms and policies. Examples of these environmental strategies include restricting the availability of alcohol, controlling prices, and promoting the responsible sales of alcohol in bars and stores (e.g., training staff to ensure that customers are at least 21 years old). Research examining these environmental strategies has shown that one of the most effective strategies to reduce alcohol consumption is to raise prices. A large meta-analysis of a 112 studies with over 1,000 estimates found significant inverse relationships between alcohol consumption or sales and measures of alcohol price and taxes (Wagenaar, Salois, and Komro, 2009). Overall, this study found that the effects of controlling the price of alcohol were comparatively larger than other prevention policies designed to reduce alcohol consumption.

Although the IOM report specifically focuses on the military, other research to prevent the onset of drinking and drug use has mostly focused on children and adolescents. Advocating a risk-focused approach, Hawkins, Catalano, and Miller (1992) suggest focusing interventions on risk and protective factors for alcohol and drug abuse. Furthermore, they contend that prevention programs should focus on these risk factors during the development period when "each begins to stabilize as a predictor of subsequent drug abuse" (p. 96). Among the various risk factors are early and persistent behavior problems, family history of alcoholism/drug abuse, academic failure, early peer rejection, and social influence on drug use. Since this early review, enough evidence has accumulated to prompt at least one review of reviews summarizing the evidence of specific risk and protective factors (Newbury-Birch et al., 2009). This narrative summary of 102 reviews highlights several risk factors for alcohol misuse. These include the following (p. 3):

- "A genetic predisposition (generational transmission);
- "Physical and sexual abuse in childhood, which may lead to later drinking behaviour;
- "Early exposure to drinking alcohol, which may increase the risk of problematic drinking in adolescence;
- "Behavioural patterns of alcohol consumption of parents, grandparents, and siblings;
- "Family history of alcohol problems;
- "Early behaviour problems in children, which may place them at especially high risk of alcohol problems, particularly if there is a family history of alcohol problems;
- "Antisocial behaviour and inter-personal problems in pre-adolescent children, which may be predictive of substance use disorders;
- "Children and young people who are sensation-seeking or have impulsive personality types may drink in large quantities;
- "Heavy and binge drinking by young people can be a mechanism for coping with stress or anxiety;
- "There may be gender differences between mothers and fathers in terms of their influence on the behaviour of sons and daughters;

- "Involvement in drinking games can lead to very high levels of alcohol consumption;
- "Mechanisms to protect children and young people, such as excessive criticism of their drinking behaviour, may not be protective but harmful;
- "Young people should be advised and supported to rely less on alcohol to facilitate social integration with their peers and to develop other more constructive peer group relationships."

Several protective factors were also noted: (pp. 3–4)

- "The location of a young person's first drink may be important to future alcohol misuse, children who first use alcohol in a home environment and learn about its effects from parents are less likely to misuse alcohol than those who begin drinking outside the home and experiment with peers.
- "Delaying the time of a young person's first drink may reduce the risk of harmful drinking.
- "Having adults who retain good relationships with a young person, characterised by appropriate levels of support and control, is likely to be protective.
- "Controlled alcohol use is not in itself predictive of negative outcomes.
- "Religious affiliation, especially attendance at religious services, may have a protective effect against alcohol consumption.
- "Key factors that seem to buffer the adverse effects of alcohol consumption in children and young people include informed and supportive parental guidance about alcohol and a delay in the age of initiation into drinking."

Smoking Interventions

Interventions for the treatment of tobacco dependence can be classified broadly into counseling and psychosocial interventions, medications, and systems changes. The "Clinical Practice Guidelines" published by the U.S. Department of Health and Human Services Public Health Service (2008) provides a thorough review of interventions in each of these three areas and provides specific recommendations for implementation. For psychosocial interventions, general recommendations indicate support for several clinician-directed interventions including screening for tobacco use, encouraging smokers to quit, meeting four or more times with individuals who are in the process of quitting, and having interventions provided through different types of clinicians (e.g., nurse, physician, health educator). Consistent with these guidelines, a Cochrane review (that is, a systematic review of primary research specifically focused on health care) of 17 randomized controlled trials (RCTs) found that providing simple advice is effective in helping people quit. The review also evaluated nine RCTs and found telephone quit lines to be effective (Mahvan et al., 2011). Evidence has also been provided for a variety of different treatment formats including telephone, individual, and group counseling, with additional support for using multiple formats. Furthermore, a recent meta-analysis of RCTs provides sufficient support for the use of Web- and computer-based interventions (Myung et al., 2009). Many of the counseling and psychosocial interventions used to treat tobacco dependence are grounded in well-researched principles from social, cognitive, and behavioral psychology.

The Cochrane review mentioned above also evaluated nicotine replacement therapies and found that bupropion, nortriptyline, clonidine, and varenicline are all effective at helping people to quit smoking (Mahvan et al., 2011). Although these treatments were found to be effective, not enough evidence is currently available to determine their relative effectiveness. This review further suggests that these medication interventions should be combined with psychosocial interventions. That is, combining counseling interventions with medication has shown to be even more effective in helping individuals to quit smoking. On a system level, there is also some evidence to indicate that clinicians should receive training in treating tobacco dependence and on how to motivate individuals who might be unwilling to quit.

Prevention of Smoking

In addition to these treatment interventions, other efforts have focused more specifically on prevention. The Committee on Smoking Cessation in Military and Veteran Populations (Bondurant and Wedge, 2009) recently reviewed several broad strategies in both civilian and military populations that target prevention. Building on recommendations provided by the CDC (2007), the committee recommends communication interventions to provide education on the consequences of tobacco use, increase knowledge of available tobacco cessation programs, and modify social norms regarding tobacco use and cessation. On a policy level, establishing smoking restrictions and tobacco-free policies, including bans, has found to be an effective strategy in reducing smoking rates. Another effective policy to influence both the initiation and cessation of smoking is by raising the price of tobacco products. This is an important point as "DoD sells tobacco products at its commissaries and exchanges, typically below the prices of the same products sold commercially outside military installations" (Bondurant and Wedge, 2009, p. 130.

7. Conclusion

This report has focused on the behavioral domain of the TFF concept. This domain focuses on specific components of behavioral health that emphasize an individual's responsibility to engage in behaviors and activities that facilitate the maintenance of health or prevent disease or dysfunction (Matarazzo, 1980). The report focuses on sleep, drug and alcohol use, and smoking.[16] Failure to appropriately manage these behaviors can lead one to be more susceptible to the negative effects of stress. Although we include research conducted with military populations, much of the research and conclusions were drawn from research with civilians. Additional research may be needed to ensure that specific findings generalize to military personnel. Nonetheless, our review of the research literature should serve as a broad foundation on which to review existing measures and initiatives used by the Air Force to promote behavioral fitness.

For each behavioral health domain, two types of measures are typically available, self-report (e.g., questionnaires) and direct measures (e.g., breathalyzer). Although direct measures overcome some of the limitations of inaccurate self-reports, their use can be limited in population studies, since they are more expensive, invasive, and time-consuming to administer. Consequently, many Air Force programs will need to rely heavily on self-report measures to track behavioral fitness. Before implementing self-report measures, the Air Force is encouraged to examine the accuracy of self-reports against direct measures with their target populations. In addition to these broad recommendations, more specific findings were associated with each behavioral domain.

Optimal functioning, from a health and well-being perspective, requires sleep. Sleep deprivation has been linked to poorer physical, psychological, and cognitive functioning, reducing a person's ability to adapt to stress. Excessive sleep loss has even been linked to such chronic diseases as cardiovascular disease and diabetes. Inadequate sleep has also been linked to poor emotional regulation, although the exact mechanism is unknown. Individuals with chronic insomnia have higher odds of developing an anxiety disorder. Sleep deprivation is associated with slower reaction time and decreased hand-eye coordination and accuracy; this effect on cognitive and motor performance is similar to that of intoxication from alcohol. Inadequate sleep also impairs problem-solving ability and decisionmaking. Several measures currently exist to assess quality and quantity of

---

[16] Other behavioral health topics such as physical activity and obesity are addressed in companion reports in this series.

sleep, including those that measure physiology during sleep (e.g., the MSLT, the PVT, actigraphs) and self-report questionnaires about sleep habits.

Although moderate drinking is believed to have some health benefits, excessive drinking is deleterious to health, well-being, readiness, and productivity. Inappropriate alcohol use has been linked to accidents and chronic disease (e.g., liver disease, cardiovascular disease, stroke). Alcohol and drug use disorders are of particular concern because a person comes to need more and more of the substance to achieve the desired physical and psychological state. Drug and alcohol use/abuse can be determined via physiological means (e.g., breathalyzers, blood test) or self-report questionnaires about drug and alcohol use behaviors.

Tobacco use is the cause of many preventable health conditions including cancer, respiratory disease, pulmonary disease, and oral disease. Smoking itself, as well as smoking cessation, has actually been associated with higher stress levels. Stress has also been implicated in relapse and continuation of smoking behaviors. Smoking also impairs physical strength and endurance and has been related to increased risk of injuries and accidents, as well as lost work days. The most common way to measure tobacco use is via self-reported questionnaires.

Clearly established interventions and prevention strategies have been developed for health behaviors, including those related to sleep, tobacco, alcohol, and substance abuse. Those programs and interventions that show the strongest evidence are multimodal in delivery and target multiple levels simultaneously (e.g., individual, family, clinicians, policymakers) and promote education as well as specific behavioral change. The adoption of any intervention or promotion program should follow up with site-specific evaluations to ensure its effectiveness in meeting program objectives for targeted populations and sites in the Air Force. Finally, it should be noted that not all factors related to health behaviors are sensitive to an intervention. For example, the positive relationship between education and health behaviors has been linked to several underlying factors including income, health insurance, family background, social networks, and factual knowledge (Cutler and Lleras-Muney, 2010). Some of these factors are intractable, suggesting that program success may be defined by modest rather than drastic changes in health behaviors.

References

Air Force Instruction 44-120, *Military Drug Demand Reduction Program,* January 3, 2011.

Alspach, G., "Napping on the Night Shift: Slacker or Savior?" *Critical Care Nurse,* Vol. 28, No. 6, 2008, pp. 12–19.

Alvarez, G. G., and N. T. Ayas, "The Impact of Daily Sleep Duration on Health: A Review of the Literature," *Progress in Cardiovascular Nursing,* Vol. 19, No. 2, 2004, pp. 56–59.

American Academy of Sleep Medicine, *ICSD—International Classification of Sleep Disorders—Revised: Diagnostic and Coding Manual,* 2001.

American Psychiatric Association, *The Diagnostic and Statistical Manual of Mental Disorders: DSM IV,* bookpointUS, 2010.

Arora, V. M., E. Georgitis, J. N. Woodruff, H. J. Humphrey, and D. Meltzer, "Improving Sleep Hygiene of Medical Interns—Can the Sleep, Alertness, and Fatigue Education in Residency Program Help?" *Archives of Internal Medicine,* Vol. 167, No. 16, September 10, 2007, pp. 1738–1744.

Balkin, T. J., P. D. Bliese, G. Belenky, H. Sing, D. R. Thorne, M. Thomas, D. P. Redmond, M. Russo, and N. J. Wesensten, "Comparative Utility of Instruments for Monitoring Sleepiness-Related Performance Decrements in the Operational Environment," *Journal of Sleep Research,* Vol. 13, No. 3, 2004, pp. 219–227.

Barber, L. K., D. C. Munz, P. G. Bagsby, and E. D. Powell, "Sleep Consistency and Sufficiency: Are Both Necessary for Less Psychological Strain?" *Stress and Health,* Vol. 26, No. 3, August 2010, pp. 186–193.

Bell, N. S., P. J. Amoroso, M. M. Yore, G. S. Smith, and B. H. Jones, "Self-Reported Risk-Taking Behaviors and Hospitalization for Motor Vehicle Injury Among Active Duty Army Personnel," *American Journal of Preventive Medicine,* Vol. 18, No. 3, 2000, pp. 85–95.

Berglund, M., S. Thelander, M. Salaspuro, J. Franck, S. Andreasson, and A. Ojehagen, "Treatment of Alcohol Abuse: An Evidence-Based Review," *Alcoholism: Clinical and Experimental Research,* Vol. 27, No. 10, October 2003, pp. 1645–1656.

Blume, A. W., K. B. Schmaling, and M. L. Russell, "Stress and Alcohol Use Among Soldiers Assessed at Mobilization and Demobilization," *Military Medicine,* Vol. 175, No. 6, June 2010, pp. 400–404.

Bondurant, S., and R. Wedge, eds., *Combating Tobacco Use in Military and Veteran Populations,* Washington, D.C.: National Academies Press, 2009.

Borges, G., C. J. Cherpitel, R. Orozco, J. Bond, Y. Ye, S. Macdonald, N. Giesbrecht, T. Stockwell, M. Cremonte, J. Moskalewicz, G. Swiatkiewicz, and V. Poznyak, "Acute Alcohol Use and the Risk of Non-Fatal Injury in Sixteen Countries," *Addiction,* Vol. 101, No. 7, July 2006, pp. 993–1002.

Bradley, K. A., A. F. DeBenedetti, R. J. Volk, E. C. Williams, D. Frank, and D. R. Kivlahan, "AUDIT-C as a Brief Screen for Alcohol Misuse in Primary Care," *Alcoholism: Clinical and Experimental Research,* Vol. 31, No. 7, July 2007, pp. 1208–1217.

Bray, R. M., M. R. Pemberton, L. L. Hourani, M. Witt, K. L. Olmsted, J. M. Brown, B. Weimer, M. E. Lance, M. E. Marsden, and S. Scheffler, *Department of Defense Survey of Health Related Behaviors Among Active Duty Military Personnel*, Research Triangle Park, N.C.: Research Triangle Inst., RTI/10940-FR, 2009.

Bray, R. M., M. R. Pemberton, M. E. Lane, L. L. Hourani, M. J. Mattiko, and L. A. Babeu, "Substance Use and Mental Health Trends Among US Military Active Duty Personnel: Key Findings from the 2008 DoD Health Behavior Survey," *Military Medicine,* Vol. 175, No. 6, June 2010a, pp. 390–399.

Bray, R. M., J. L. Spira, K. R. Olmsted, and J. J. Hout, "Behavioral and Occupational Fitness," *Military Medicine,* Vol. 175, (Supplement 1), 2010b, pp. 39–56.

Breslau, N., S. P. Novak, and R. C. Kessler, "Daily Smoking and the Subsequent Onset of Psychiatric Disorders," *Psychological Medicine,* Vol. 34, No. 2, February 2004, pp. 323–333.

Brown, F. C., W. C. Buboltz, and B. Soper, "Relationship of Sleep Hygiene Awareness, Sleep Hygiene Practices, and Sleep Quality in University sStudents," *Behavioral Medicine,* Vol. 28, No. 1, 2002, pp. 33–38.

Buysse, D. J., C. F. Reynolds III, T. H. Monk, S. R. Berman, and D. J. Kupfer, "The Pittsburgh Sleep Quality Index: A New Instrument for Psychiatric Practice and Research," *Psychiatry Research,* Vol. 28, No. 2, 1989, pp. 193–213.

Cappuccio, F. P., L. D'Elia, P. Strazzullo, and M. A. Miller, "Sleep Duration and All-Cause Mortality: A Systematic Review and Meta-Analysis of Prospective Studies," *Sleep,* Vol. 33, No. 5, May 2010, pp. 585–592.

Carroll, K. M., *A Cognitive-Behavioral Approach: Treating Cocaine Addiction,* NIH Publication 98-4308, Rockville, Md: National Institute on Drug Abuse, 1998.

Carroll, K. M., and L. S. Onken, "Behavioral Therapies for Drug Abuse," *American Journal of Psychiatry,* Vol. 162, No. 8, August 2005, pp. 1452–1460.

CDC—*See* Centers for Disease Control and Prevention.

Centers for Disease Control and Prevention, "Sleep and Sleep Disorders," September 23, 2010. As of January 30, 2014:
http://www.cdc.gov/Features/Sleep/

———, *Best Practices for Comprehensive Tobacco Control Programs—2007,* Atlanta, Ga.: Office on Smoking and Health, 2007.

Chen, P. H., H. Y. Kuo, and K. H. Chueh, "Sleep Hygiene Education: Efficacy on Sleep Quality in Working Women," *Journal of Nursing Research,* Vol. 18, No. 4, 2010, p. 283.

Cherpitel, C. J., "Screening for Alcohol Problems in the US General Population: Comparison of the CAGE, RAPS4, and RAPS4-QF by Gender, Ethnicity, and Service Utilization," *Alcoholism: Clinical and Experimental Research,* Vol. 26, No. 11, 2002, pp. 1686–1691.

Cook, R. T., "Alcohol Abuse, Alcoholism, and Damage to the Immune System—A Review," *Alcoholism: Clinical and Experimental Research,* Vol. 22, No. 9, 1998, pp. 1927–1942.

Cutler, D. M., and A. Lleras-Muney, "Understanding Differences in Health Behaviors by Education," *Journal of Health Economics,* Vol. 29, No. 1, January 2010, pp. 1–28.

Davies, K. A., G. J. Macfarlane, B. I. Nicholl, C. Dickens, R. Morriss, D. Ray, and J. McBeth, "Restorative Sleep Predicts the Resolution of Chronic Widespread Pain: Results from the EPIFUND Study," *Rheumatology,* Vol. 47, No. 12, December 2008, pp. 1809–1813.

Dawson, D. A., R. B. Goldstein, S. P. Chou, W. J. Ruan, and B. F. Grant, "Age at First Drink and the First Incidence of Adult-Onset DSM-IV Alcohol Use Disorders," *Alcoholism: Clinical and Experimental Research,* Vol. 32, No. 12, December 2008, pp. 2149–2160.

Dawson, D. A., B. F. Grant, and T. K. Li, "Impact of Age at First Drink on Stress-Reactive Drinking," *Alcoholism: Clinical and Experimental Research,* Vol. 31, No. 1, January 2007, pp. 69–77.

Dawson, D. A., B. F. Grant, F. S. Stinson, and Y. Zhou, "Effectiveness of the Derived Alcohol Use Disorders Identification Test (AUDIT-C) in Screening for Alcohol Use Disorders and Risk Drinking in the US General Population," *Alcoholism: Clinical and Experimental Research,* Vol. 29, No. 5, May 2005, pp. 844–854.

DCoE—*See* Defense Centers of Excellence.

Defense Centers of Excellence for Psychological Health and Traumatic Brain Injury (DCoE), *Traumatic Brain Injury,* 2011. As of January 31,2014:
http://www.dcoe.health.mil/Content/Navigation/Documents/About%20TBI.pdf

Department of Defense Directive 1010.4, "Drug and Alcohol Abuse by DoD Personnel," September 3, 1997, as amended; subsequently replaced by DoD Directive 1010.04, "Problematic Substance Use by DoD Personnel," February 20, 2014.

Department of Defense Instruction (DoDI) 1010.16, *Technical Procedures for the Military Personnel Drug Abuse Testing Program,* Decemer 9, 1994.

DeWit, D. J., E. M. Adlaf, D. R. Offord, and A. C. Ogborne, "Age at First Alcohol Use: A Risk Factor for the Development of Alcohol Disorders," *American Journal of Psychiatry,* Vol. 157, No. 5, May 2000, pp. 745–750.

Dinges, D., and J. Powell, "Microcomputer Analyses of Performance on a Portable, Simple Visual RT Task During Sustained Operations," *Behavior Research Methods,* Vol. 17, No. 6, 1985, pp. 652–655.

DoDI—*See* Department of Defense Instruction.

Donovan, J. E., "Estimated Blood Alcohol Concentrations for Child and Adolescent Drinking and Their Implications for Screening Instruments," *Pediatrics,* Vol. 123, No. 6, June 2009, pp. e975–e981.

Dutra, L., G. Stathopoulou, S. L. Basden, T. M. Leyro, M. B. Powers, and M. W. Otto, "A Meta-Analytic Review of Psychosocial Interventions for Substance Use Disorders," *American Journal of Psychiatry,* Vol. 165, No. 2, February 2008, pp. 179–187.

Dyer, F. N., *Smoking and Soldier Performance: A Literature Review*, Columbus, Ga.: Research Solutions, Inc., U.S. Army Aeromedical Research Laboratory, 1986.

Enoch, M. A., "The Role of Early Life Stress as a Predictor for Alcohol and Drug Dependence," *Psychopharmacology,* Vol. 214, No. 1, March 2011, pp. 17–31.

Ewing, J. A., "Detecting Alcoholism. The CAGE questionnaire," *JAMA: The Journal of the American Medical Association,* Vol. 252, No. 14, October 12, 1984, pp. 1905–1907.

Flórez, K. R., R. A. Shih, and M. T. Martin, *Nutritional Fitness and Resilience: A Review of Relevant Constructs, Measures, and Links to Well-Being,* Santa Monica, Calif.: RAND Corporation, RR-105-AF, 2014. As of September 30, 2014: http://www.rand.org/pubs/research_reports/RR105.html

Friedl, K. E., and D. M. Penetar, "Resilience and Survival in Extreme Environments," in B. J. Lukey and V. Tepe, eds., *Biobehavioral Resilience to Stress,* Boca Raton, Fla.: CRC Press, 2008, pp. 139–176.

Gallant, M. P., and G. P. Dorn, "Gender and Race differences in the Predictors of Daily Health Practices Among Older Adults," *Health Education Research,* Vol. 16, No. 1, 2001, p. 21.

Gorber, S. C., S. Schofield-Hurwitz, J. Hardt, G. Levasseur, and M. Tremblay, "The Accuracy of Self-Reported Smoking: A Systematic Review of the Relationship Between Self-Reported and Cotinine-Assessed Smoking Status," *Nicotine & Tobacco Research,* Vol. 11, No. 1, January 2009, pp. 12–24.

Haddock, C. K., R. C. Klesges, G. W. Talcott, H. Lando, and R. J. Stein, "Smoking Prevalence and Risk Factors for Smoking in a Population of United States Air Force Basic Trainees," *Tobacco Control,* Vol. 7, No. 3, Autumn 1998, pp. 232–235.

Hamilton, N. A., D. Catley, and C. Karlson, "Sleep and the Affective Response to Stress and Pain," *Health Psychology,* Vol. 26, No. 3, May 2007, pp. 288–295.

Hawkins, J. D., R. F. Catalano, and J. Y. Miller, "Risk and Protective Factors for Alcohol and Other Drug Problems in Adolescence and Early Adulthood—Implications for Substance-Abuse Prevention," *Psychological Bulletin,* Vol. 112, No. 1, July 1992, pp. 64–105.

Institute of Medicine, *Substance Use Disorders in the U.S. Armed Forces.* Washington, D.C.: The National Academies Press, 2013.

IOM—*See* Institute of Medicine.

Jaffee, W. B., E. Trucco, S. Levy, and R. D. Weiss, "Is This Urine Really Negative? A Systematic Review of Tampering Methods in Urine Drug Screening and Testing," *Journal of Substance Abuse Treatment,* Vol. 33, No. 1, July 2007, pp. 33–42.

Jeffery, D. D., L. A. Babeu, L. E. Nelson, M. Kloc, and K. Klette, "Prescription Drug Misuse Among US Active Duty Military Personnel: A Secondary Analysis of the 2008 DoD Survey of Health Related Behaviors," *Military Medicine,* Vol. 178, No. 2, 2013, pp. 180–195.

Kassel, J. D., L. R. Stroud, and C. A. Paronis, "Smoking, Stress, and Negative Affect: Correlation, Causation, and Context Across Stages of Smoking," *Psychological Bulletin,* Vol. 129, No. 2, March 2003, pp. 270–304.

Kelly, T. M., J. E. Donovan, J. M. Kinnane, and D.M.C.D. Taylor, "A Comparison of Alcohol Screening Instruments Among Under-Aged Drinkers Treated in Emergency Departments," *Alcohol and Alcoholism,* Vol. 37, No. 5, 2002, p. 444.

Kessler, R. C., "The National Comorbidity Survey: Preliminary Results and Future Directions," *International Journal of Methods in Psychiatric Research*, Vol. 5, 1995, pp. 139–151.

Killgore, W. D., T. J. Balkin, and N. J. Wesensten, "Impaired Decision Making Following 49 h of Sleep Deprivation," *Journal of Sleep Research,* Vol. 15, No. 1, March 2006, pp. 7–13.

Killgore, W.D.S., E. T. Kahn-Greene, E. L. Lipizzi, R. A. Newman, G. H. Kamimori, and T. J. Balkin, "Sleep Deprivation Reduces Perceived Emotional Intelligence and Constructive Thinking Skills," *Sleep Medicine,* Vol. 9, No. 5, 2008, pp. 517–526.

Koffel, E., and D. Watson, "The Two-Factor Structure of Sleep Complaints and Its Relation to Depression and Anxiety," *Journal of Abnormal Psychology,* Vol. 118, No. 1, 2009, p. 183.

LeBourgeois, M. K., F. Giannotti, F. Cortesi, A. R. Wolfson, and J. Harsh, "The Relationship Between Reported Sleep Quality and Sleep Hygiene in Italian and American Adolescents," *Pediatrics,* Vol. 115 (Supplement), 2005, p. 257.

Linde, L., and M. Bergstrom, "The Effect of One Night Without Sleep on Problem-Solving and Immediate Recall," *Psychological Research,* Vol. 54, No. 2, 1992, pp. 127–136.

Mahvan, T., R. Namdar, K. Voorhees, P. C. Smith, and W. Ackerman, "Clinical Inquiry: Which Smoking Cessation Interventions Work Best?" *The Journal of Family Practice,* Vol. 60, No. 7, July 2011, pp. 430–431.

Marcus, S. E., G. A. Giovino, J. P. Pierce, and Y. Harel, "Measuring Tobacco Use among Adolescents," *Public Health Reports,* Vol. 108, 1993, pp. 20–24.

Marlatt, G. A., and J. R. Gordon, *Relapse Prevention: Maintenance Strategies in the Treatment of Addictive Behaviors*, The Guilford Clinical Psychology and Psychotherapy Series, New York: Guilford Press, 1985.

Matarazzo, J. D., "Behavioral Health and Behavioral Medicine—Frontiers for a New Health Psychology," *American Psychologist,* Vol. 35, No. 9, 1980, pp. 807–817.

Mattiko, M. J., K. L. R. Olmsted, J. M. Brown, and R. M. Bray, "Alcohol Use and Negative Consequences Among Active Duty Military Personnel," *Addictive Behaviors,* Vol. 36, No. 6, June 2011, pp. 608–614.

McCabe, S. E., J. A. Cranford, and B. T. West, "Trends in Prescription Drug Abuse and Dependence, Co-Occurrence with Other Substance Use Disorders, and Treatment Utilization: Results from Two National Surveys," *Addictive Behaviors,* Vol. 33, No. 10, October 2008, pp. 1297–1305.

McGene, J., *Social Fitness and Resilience: A Review of Relevant Constructs, Measures, and Links to Well-Being,* Santa Monica, Calif.: RAND Corporation, RR-108-AF, 2013. As of October 3, 2013:
http://www.rand.org/pubs/research_reports/RR108.html

McLay, R. N., W. P. Klam, and S. L. Volkert, "Insomnia Is the Most Commonly Reported Symptom and Predicts Other Symptoms of Post-Traumatic Stress Disorder in U.S. Service Members Returning from Military Deployments," *Military Medicine,* Vol. 175, No. 10, October 2010, pp. 759–762.

Meadows, S. O., and L. L. Miller, *Airman and Family Resilience: Lessons from the Scientific Literature,* Santa Monica, Calif.: RAND Corporation, RR-106-AF, forthcoming.

Mitler, M. M., M. A. Carskadon, C. A. Czeisler, W. C. Dement, D. F. Dinges, and R. C. Graeber, "Catastrophes, Sleep, and Public Policy: Consensus Report," *Sleep,* Vol. 11, No. 1, 1988, p. 100.

Moberg, C. A., and J. J. Curtin, "Alcohol Selectively Reduces Anxiety but Not Fear: Startle Response During Unpredictable Versus Predictable Threat," *Journal of Abnormal Psychology,* Vol. 118, No. 2, May 2009, pp. 335–347.

Morin, C. M., J. P. Culbert, and S. M. Schwartz, "Nonpharmacological Interventions for Insomnia: A Meta-Analysis of Treatment Efficacy," *American Journal of Psychiatry,* Vol. 151, No. 8, 1994, p. 1172.

Mullen, Admiral M., "On Total Force Fitness in War and Peace," *Military Medicine,* Vol. 175 (Supplement), 2010, pp. 1–2.

Murtagh, D.R.R., and K. M. Greenwood, "Identifying Effective Psychological Treatments for Insomnia: A Meta-Analysis," *Journal of Consulting and Clinical Psychology*, Vol. 63, No. 1, 1995, p. 79.

Myllymaki, T., H. Kyrolainen, K. Savolainen, L. Hokka, R. Jakonen, T. Juuti, K. Martinmaki, J. Kaartinen, M. L. Kinnunen, and H. Rusko, "Effects of Vigorous Late-Night Exercise on Sleep Quality and Cardiac Autonomic Activity," *Journal of Sleep Research,* Vol. 20, No. 1, March 2011, pp. 146–153.

Myung, S. K., D. D. McDonnell, G. Kazinets, H. G. Seo, and J. M. Moskowitz, "Effects of Web- and Computer-Based Smoking Cessation Programs Meta-analysis of Randomized Controlled Trials," *Archives of Internal Medicine,* Vol. 169, No. 10, May 25, 2009, pp. 929–937.

National Heart, Lung, and Blood Institute, "What Are Sleep Studies?" March 29, 2012. As of January 28, 2014:
http://www.nhlbi.nih.gov/health/dci/Diseases/slpst/slpst_types.html

National Institute on Alcohol Abuse and Alcoholism Task Force on Recommended Alcohol Questions, "Recommended Alcohol Questions," October 2003. As of May 14, 2014:
http://www.niaaa.nih.gov/research/guidelines-and-resources/recommended-alcohol-questions

National Institute on Alcohol Abuse and Alcoholism, "NIAAA Council Approves Definition of Binge Drinking," 2004.

National Institutes of Health; National Heart, Lung, and Blood Institute; and National Center on Sleep Disorders, *Research Guide to Selected Publicly Available Sleep-Related Data Resources*, July 2006.

National Institutes on Drug Abuse, "Principles of Drug Addiction Treatment: A Research-Based Guide," 3rd ed., Rockville, Md.: NIDA, 2012.

National Research Council, *Promoting Health: Intervention Strategies from Social and Behavioral Research*, Washington, D.C.: The National Academies Press, 2000.

———, *Combating Tobacco Use in Military and Veteran Populations*, Washington, D.C.: The National Academies Press, 2009.

National Sleep Foundation, "Can't Sleep, What to Know About Insomnia," undated. As of January 30, 2014:
http://www.sleepfoundation.org/article/sleep-related-problems/insomnia-and-sleep

Neckelmann, D., A. Mykletun, and A. A. Dahl, "Chronic Insomnia as a Risk Factor for Developing Anxiety and Depression," *Sleep,* Vol. 30, No. 7, 2007, p. 873.

Newbury-Birch, D., E. Gilvarry, P. McArdle, V. Ramesh, S. Stewart, J. Walker, L. Avery, F. Beyer, N. Brown, and K. Jackson, "Impact of Alcohol Consumption on Young People: A Review of Reviews," Newcastle University, U.K.: Institute of Health and Society, 2009.

NIAAA—*See* National Institute on Alcohol Abuse and Alcoholism.

Noar, S. M., C. N. Benac, and M. S. Harris, "Does Tailoring Matter? Meta-Analytic Review of Tailored Print Health Behavior Change Interventions," *Psychological Bulletin,* Vol. 133, No. 4, July 2007, pp. 673–693.

Noonan, D., Y. Y. Jiang, and S. A. Duffy, "Utility of Biochemical Verification of Tobacco Cessation in the Department of Veterans Affairs," *Addictive Behaviors,* Vol. 38, No. 3, March 2013, pp. 1792–1795.

Orasanu, J. M., and P. Backer, "Stress and Military Performance," in J. E. Driskell and E. Salas, eds., *Stress and Human Performance,* Mahwah, N.J.: Lawrence Erlbaum Associates, 1996, pp. 89–126.

Ozer, O., B. Ozbala, I. Sari, V. Davutoglu, E. Maden, Y. Baltaci, S. Yavuz, and M. Aksoy, "Acute Sleep Deprivation Is Associated with Increased QT Dispersion in Healthy Young Adults," *Pace-Pacing and Clinical Electrophysiology,* Vol. 31, No. 8, August 2008, pp. 979–984.

Pallesen, S., M. Mitsem, G. Kvale, B. H. Johnsen, and H. Molde, "Outcome of Psychological Treatments of Pathological Gambling: A Review and Meta Analysis," *Addiction,* Vol. 100, No. 10, 2005, pp. 1412–1422.

Parrott, A. C., "Does Cigarette Smoking Cause Stress?" *American Psychologist,* Vol. 54, No. 10, October 1999, pp. 817–820.

Patel, S. R., and F. B. Hu, "Short Sleep Duration and Weight Gain: A Systematic Review," *Obesity,* Vol. 16, No. 3, 2008, pp. 643–653.

Patel, S. R., A. Malhotra, D. J. Gottlieb, D. P. White, and F. B, Hu, "Correlates of Long Sleep Duration," *Sleep,* Vol. 29, No. 7, 2006, pp. 881–889.

Perlis, M. L., D. E. Giles, W. B. Mendelson, R. R. Bootzin, and J. K. Wyatt, "Psychophysiological Insomnia: The Behavioural Model and a Neurocognitive Perspective," *Journal of Sleep Research,* Vol. 6, No. 3, 1997, pp. 179–188.

Peterson, A. L., J. L. Goodie, W. A. Satterfield, and W. L. Brim, "Sleep Disturbance During Military Deployment," *Military Medicine,* Vol. 173, No. 3, March 2008, pp. 230–235.

Rechtschaffen, A., "Current Perspectives on the Function of Sleep," *Perspectives in Biology and Medicine,* Vol. 41, No. 3, Spring 1998, pp. 359–390.

Redwine, L., R. L. Hauger, J. C. Gillin, and M. Irwin, "Effects of Sleep and Sleep Deprivation on Interleukin-6, Growth Hormone, Cortisol, and Melatonin Levels in Humans," *Journal of Clinical Endocrinology & Metabolism,* Vol. 85, No. 10, 2000, p. 3597.

Robson, S., *Physical Fitness and Resilience: A Review of Relevant Constructs, Measures, and Links to Well-Being,* Santa Monica, Calif.: RAND Corporation, RR-104-AF, 2013. As of October 3, 2013:
http://www.rand.org/pubs/research_reports/RR104.html

———, *Psychological Fitness and Resilience: A Review of Relevant Constructs, Measures, and Links to Well-Being,* Santa Monica, Calif.: RAND Corporation, RR-102-AF, 2014. As of March 11, 2014:
http://www.rand.org/pubs/research_reports/RR102.html

Robson, S., and N. Salcedo, *Behavioral Fitness and Resilience: A Review of Relevant Constructs, Measures, and Links to Well-Being,* Santa Monica, Calif.: RAND Corporation, RR-103-AF, 2014. As of December 2014:
http://www.rand.org/pubs/research_reports/RR103.html

Roehrs, T., and T. Roth, "Sleep, Sleepiness, and Alcohol Use," *Alcohol Research & Health,* Vol. 25, No. 2, 2001, pp. 101–109.

Rothman, E. F., W. DeJong, T. Palfai, and R. Saitz, "Relationship of Age of First Drink to Alcohol-Related Consequences Among College Students with Unhealthy Alcohol Use," *Substance Abuse,* Vol. 29, No. 1, 2008, pp. 33–41.

SAMHSA—*See* Substance Abuse and Mental Health Services Administration.

Saunders, J. B., O. G. Aasland, T. F. Babor, J. R. Delafuente, and M. Grant, "Development of the Alcohol-Use Disorders Identification Test (Audit)—WHO Collaborative Project on Early Detection of Persons with Harmful Alcohol-Consumption-II," *Addiction,* Vol. 88, No. 6, June 1993, pp. 791–804.

Sher, K. J., B. D. Bartholow, K. Peuser, D. J. Erickson, and M. D. Wood, "Stress-Response-Dampening Effects of Alcohol: Attention as a Mediator and Moderator," *Journal of Abnormal Psychology,* Vol. 116, No. 2, May 2007, pp. 362–377.

43

Shih, R. A., S. O. Meadows, and M. T. Martin, *Medical Fitness and Resilience: A Review of Relevant Constructs, Measures, and Links to Well-Being,* Santa Monica, Calif.: RAND Corporation, RR-107-AF, 2013. As of October 3, 2013: http://www.rand.org/pubs/research_reports/RR107.html

Shih, R. A., S. O. Meadows, J. Mendeloff, and K. Bowling, *Environmental Fitness and Resilience: A Review of Relevant Constructs, Measures, and Links to Well-Being,* Santa Monica, Calif.: RAND Corporation, RR-101-AF, forthcoming.

Sinha, R., "How Does Stress Increase Risk of Drug Abuse and Relapse?" *Psychopharmacology,* Vol. 158, No. 4, December 2001, pp. 343–359.

Sinha, R., "Chronic Stress, Drug Use, and Vulnerability to Addiction," *Addiction Reviews 2008,* Vol. 1141, 2008, pp. 105–130.

Skinner, H. A., "The Drug Abuse Screening Test," *Addictive Behaviors,* Vol. 7, No. 4, 1982, pp. 363–371.

Smedslund, G., R. C. Berg, K. T. Hammerstrøm, A. Steiro, K. A. Leiknes, H. M. Dahl, and K. Karlsen, " Motivational Interviewing for Substance Abuse," Cochrane database of systematic reviews (Online), No. 11, 2011.

Smit, E., J. Verdurmen, K. Monshouwer, and F. Smit, "Family Interventions and Their Effect on Adolescent Alcohol Use in General Populations; A Meta-Analysis of Randomized Controlled Trials," *Drug and Alcohol Dependence,* Vol. 97, No. 3, October 1, 2008, pp. 195–206.

Smith, M. T., M. L. Perlis, A. Park, M. S. Smith, J. M. Pennington, D. E. Giles, and D. J. Buysse, "Comparative Meta-Analysis of Pharmacotherapy and Behavior Therapy for Persistent Insomnia," *American Journal of Psychiatry,* Vol. 159, No. 1, 2002, p. 5.

Spera, C., R. K. Thomas, F. Barlas, R. Szoc, and M. H. Cambridge, "Relationship of Military Deployment Recency, Frequency, Duration, and Combat Exposure to Alcohol Use in the Air Force," *Journal of Studies on Alcohol and Drugs,* Vol. 72, No. 1, January 2011, pp. 5–14.

Stahre, M. A., R. D. Brewer, V. P. Fonseca, and T. S. Naimi, "Binge Drinking Among US Active-Duty Military Personnel," *American Journal of Preventive Medicine,* Vol. 36, No. 3, 2009, pp. 208–217.

Standards of Practice Committee of the American Academy of Sleep Medicine, "Practice Parameters for the Role of Actigraphy in the Study of Sleep and Circadian Rhythms: An Update for 2002, *Sleep,* Vol. 26, No. 3, 2003, pp. 337–341.

Stanton, M. D., and W. R. Shadish, "Outcome, Attrition, and Family Couples Treatment for Drug Abuse: A Meta-Analysis and Review of the Controlled, Comparative Studies," *Psychological Bulletin,* Vol. 122, No. 2, 1997, p. 170.

Streufert, S., R. M. Pogash, J. Roache, D. Gingrich, R. Landis, W. Severs, L. Lonardi, and A. Kantner, "Effects of Alcohol Intoxication on Risk Taking, Strategy, and Error Rate in Visuomotor Performance," *The Journal of Applied Psychology,* Vol. 77, No. 4, August 1992, pp. 515–524.

Substance Abuse and Mental Health Services Administration, "Mandatory Guidelines for Federal Workplace Drug Testing Programs," *Federal Register*, Vol. 69, 2004, pp. 19644–19673.

Thompson, J. C., T-C. Kao, and R. J. Thomas, "The Relationship Between Alcohol Use and Risk-Taking Sexual Behaviors in a Large Behavioral Study," *Preventive Medicine,* Vol. 41, No. 1, 2005, pp. 247–252.

U.S. Department of Health and Human Services, T*he Health Consequences of Smoking: A Report of the Surgeon General,* Atlanta, Ga.: Centers for Disease Control and Prevention, National Center for Chronic Disease Prevention and Health Promotion, Office on Smoking and Health, Vol. 62, 2004.

———, *Rethinking Drinking: Alcohol and Your Health,* National Institute on Alcohol Abuse and Alcoholism, NIH Publication No. 10-3770, New York, 2010.

U.S. Department of Health and Human Services Public Health Service, "Clinical Practice Guideline," *Treating Tobacco Use and Dependence: 2008 Update,* Rockville Md., 2008.

U.S. National Library of Medicine, National Institutes of Health, MedlinePlus website, "Toxicology Screen," January 12, 2011. As of June 9, 2012: http://www.nlm.nih.gov/medlineplus/ency/article/003578.htm

Veterans Administration/Department of Defense, *Clinical Practice Guideline for the Management of Tobacco Use*, prepared by Management of Tobacco Use Working Group, June 2004.

Wagenaar, A. C., M. J. Salois, and K. A. Komro, "Effects of Beverage Alcohol Price and Tax Levels on Drinking: A Meta-Analysis of 1003 Estimates from 112 Studies," *Addiction,* Vol. 104, No. 2, 2009, pp. 179–190.

Walker, M. P., and R. Stickgold, "Sleep, Memory, and Plasticity," *Annual Review of Psychology,* Vol. 57, 2006, pp. 139–166.

Walker, M. P., and E. van Der Helm, "Overnight Therapy? The Role of Sleep in Emotional Brain Processing," *Psychological Bulletin,* Vol. 135, No. 5, 2009, p. 731.

Westermeyer, J., R. J. Sutherland, M. Freerks, K. Martin, P. Thuras, D. Johnson, R. Rossom, and T. Hurwitz, "Reliability of Sleep Log Data Versus Actigraphy in Veterans with Sleep Disturbance and PTSD," *Journal of Anxiety Disorders*, Vol. 21, No. 7, 2007, pp. 966–975.

Williamson, A. M., and A. M. Feyer, "Moderate Sleep Deprivation Produces Impairments in Cognitive and Motor Performance Equivalent to Legally Prescribed Levels of Alcohol Intoxication," *Occupational and Environmental Medicine,* Vol. 57, No. 10, October 2000, pp. 649–655.

Wilsnack, R. W., N. D. Vogeltanz, S. C. Wilsnack, and T. R. Harris, "Gender Differences in Alcohol Consumption and Adverse Drinking Consequences: Cross Cultural Patterns," *Addiction,* Vol. 95, No. 2, 2000, pp. 251–265.

Wittchen, H. U., "Reliability and Validity Studies of the WHO—Composite International Diagnostic Interview (CIDI): A Critical Review," *Journal of Psychiatric Research,* Vol. 28, No. 1, January–February 1994, pp. 57–84.

Wittchen, H. U., L. N. Robins, L. B. Cottler, N. Sartorius, J. D. Burke, and D. Regier, "Cross-Cultural Feasibility, Reliability and Sources of Variance of the Composite International Diagnostic Interview (CIDI). The Multicentre WHO/ADAMHA Field Trials," *The British Journal of Psychiatry: The Journal of Mental Science,* Vol. 159, November 1991, pp. 645–653, 658.

Yeung, D., and M. T. Martin, *Spiritual Fitness and Resilience: A Review of Relevant Constructs, Measures, and Links to Well-Being,* Santa Monica, Calif.: RAND Corporation, RR-100-AF, 2013. As of October 3, 2013:
http://www.rand.org/pubs/research_reports/RR100.html

Youngstedt, S. D. , and C. E. Kline, "Epidemiology of Exercise and Sleep," *Sleep and Biological Rhythms,* Vol. 4, 2006, pp. 215–221.

Yudko, E., O. Lozhkina, and A. Fouts, "A Comprehensive Review of the Psychometric Properties of the Drug Abuse Screening Test," *Journal of Substance Abuse Treatment,* Vol. 32, No. 2, March 2007, pp. 189–198.

Ziedonis, D., B. Hitsman, J. Beckham, M. Zvolensky, L. Adler, J. Audrain-McGovern, N. Breslau, R. Brown, T. George, J. Williams, P. Calhoun, and W. Riley, "Tobacco Use and Cessation in Psychiatric Disorders: National Institute of Mental Health Report," *Nicotine & Tobacco Research,* Vol. 10, No. 12, 2008, pp. 1691–1715.